Realm of the Adventurer
Copyright © 2024 by Patrick Malyszek

First printing April 2024

Library of Congress Cataloging-in-Publication Data

Malyszek, Patrick
Realm of the Adventurer/ by Patrick Malyszek

Paperback ISBN: 978-1-965092-28-6
Hardcover ISBN: 978-1-965092-29-3

Published by AR PRESS, an American Real Publishing Company
Roger L. Brooks, Publisher
roger@incubatemedia.us
americanrealpublishing.com

Interior design by Eva Myrick, MSCP

Printed in the U.S.A.

REALM OF THE ADVENTURER

A Journey Beyond Boundaries

Patrick Malyszek

AR PRESS

Table of Contents

When my five sisters and five brothers left to watch TV after dinner, I stayed at the kitchen table lost in thought. My father asked why I was so contemplative. My mother stopped what she was doing—waiting for my answer. "Well, I am trying to figure out my path in life and determine what a realistic goal is for myself." There was a pause. *Did I say something wrong*? The silence was broken when almost at the same time both my mother and father said, "To be realistic in your goals is the first step to failure. Reach out beyond your wildest dreams and never stop chasing your unrealistic expectations." Ever since I heard those words, I've always reached beyond this world and I look upon this world differently than most. Thanks Mom and Dad, for showing me the truth.

Acknowledgments

I would like to acknowledge my brothers, sisters, and my wife for always being there for me, supporting my dreams, wild expectations, and all of the mistakes I've made during my life. Without their dedication and love I would not be known as "Patreeek." I would also like to thank my brother Wally for pushing me to write this book. He always kept me focused on getting it done, and after a few years I did. The final push came from Kathy Ferro Weiss, who gave me the courage to work with American Real Publishing and their fantastic staff of professionals.

Introduction

"Your heart and soul are never more apparent until you are alone in the wilderness."

Written by Patrick Malyszek

As a young boy I always had a notion there was another side to life, a parallel life that was available to all but only a few that were graced with the ability to acknowledge and experience it. I wanted to find this parallel life and experience what it had to offer as compared to our regular everyday life...but I did not have a clue as to how to find and experience it. I would go into the forest every day regardless of the weather and spend hours and hours just thinking and exploring, trying to determine what the trigger was in order to experience this different side of life. What I learned is that you cannot use your regular life's experiences as the trigger. In order to really reach and experience the other side of life you must have not the ability, but rather the passion and desire to be a person that is willing to break their own social norms and challenge themselves with out of control experiences. These experiences create what I call a "bridge" from our common life to the life of an adventurer, which leads into what I have termed *The Realm*. A place of true love, support, and confidence.

The transition from my common life, which is great by the way, to The Realm, which is mystic, is not an easy task and for most will never be achieved or experienced. But I made it, I found my "bridges" into The Realm. Yes! Bridges. There is not just one way to get into The Realm, there are actually hundreds of ways to get to that special place.

My "bridges" into The Realm were found not by pressuring myself, which I had done for years, but through having an open mind to all things. I recall trying so hard but always finding myself a little lost and confused. It existed—I knew that, but I could not grasp it. At times I would look to the world for the answer but knew deep inside that was wrong. Other times I would look to others for the "bridge" but every time I did that the path I was seeking was obstructed by confusion and could not be seen or felt at all. To look to others was wrong. Self-reliance is 100% critical. What was also very important was having the courage to move away from common life and try to become an adventurer that was willing to take on acts of spontaneity. To take on the unknown without fear of the outcome.

Within this book there are several true-life stories, all of which have taken me to places beyond this world, beyond myself, and to a place where I come closest to finding true love, support, spirts of the loved ones that have gone to heaven, God, and a few near death experiences in Alaska. Some of the stories that you will read include: *The Escape*, which is about finding The Realm and becoming a true adventurer. *Crashed and Broken* is when I fell off a glacier in Alaska and had to be rescued. *The Charge* is the time that I was charged by a bear. All amazing stuff for sure. All of this was done while in The Realm.

I truly hope this book and my stories give you the courage to find The Realm, and become an Adventurer in order to live a great life filled with love that is pure and of absolute truth. GOOD LUCK and CALL ME IF YOU NEED HELP!!

Story 1

The Escape

Most everyone has a dream, a dream that will take them away from their standard routines and practices of life. For some, these dreams are merely flirtatious aspirations. And for a very choice few, their dreams become a resounding reality filled with life-changing events leading to other dreams and inspirations that grow into new adventures. So, take the time to slow down during the day and think about what you want to do, see, and experience. Think about it nonstop. Does that make you feel good? Does it make you feel free? Does it give you inspiration to work harder while on the clock? Get serious!!! To merely have a dream is the easiest way of running away from what you really want, because dreamers have a fear of reality when it comes to making a dream come true. This fear is rooted in changing one's routine and practices. This is not easy, as routines create a sense of false security by seeing and doing the same old thing every day. 'If I can predict the future, I can control the future.' This is the basis as to why so many dreamers never take the chance to transform a dream into reality. Ask yourself, what do you want out of life? Do you want to be free? Do you want the excitement of not knowing what will happen next? Are you willing to enter your dream with unbridled spontaneity, allowing it to meet the unexpected challenges of not knowing what is coming next? Well, answer the damn questions! I answered yes to these questions because I wanted to be more than a dreamer, I wanted to be an adventurer inspired by my dreams.

Become an adventurer! That is what I really wanted. But wait—at this point I did not have a dream upon which to rely. No problem, I told myself—*I will go to bed on this night, lie down, and dream a dream or two, select one, and then become a true adventurer.* On this night, I did not have one single dream, but I did get a chance to count the number of holes in the ceiling tiles. No worries! *So, I will just wait until tomorrow night and have a spectacular dream of conquering a high mountain spire without any rope.* Great! If I have that dream, I will become a mountain climber. The best in the world. I am scared of heights! Okay, it's night number two. It's time for a reload.

OOOOOH man, another night with no stinking dream. Am I really that boring that my subconscious mind cannot even conjure up a simple dream? At this point, I would settle for a dream about anything. Well, maybe not *anything*! So, on this morning I get ready for work to ensure that I get to my desk no later than 8:00 a.m. I have to admit, my morning routine did give me a sense of unrealistic security. So maybe I wouldn't become an adventurer, maybe I should just settle for who I am. A boring office worker, pushing paper and agreeing to everything his boss says. She is a tough boss too, but fair and reasonable. I don't really mean that, but just in case she reads this story, I have a rebuttable defense.

One thing that I cannot tolerate is sitting in front of my computer all day. I need to get up and look out the windows to let my eyes refocus. Going to the windows has become a pastime that we at my office call MWMs (Mandatory Window Meetings). We have these meetings several times a day at work. The attendees are always looking out the window, engaging in small talk about random things, such as making comments about people walking by, the weather, and people trying to parallel park their cars. There are a lot of bad drivers out there. One time this person was trying to parallel park and hit the car in front of them three times. We have watched drivers roll onto the curb, and some actually leave their cars partially in the road. It is a scary world out there. We have so many MWMs that we are recognized by people in the neighborhood. Across the street there is a medical office, and on more than one occasion the doctor came out of his office and threw his hands up gesturing to all of the window watchers to get back to work. There are even a few people who drive by in their cars that know enough to look up to the second floor windows and wave. We now have a new friend. A banker that works at Key Bank across the street. Every time he comes out of the bank, he looks up and waves. He comes out so many times that it is easy to see he is taking his own personal MWM. Actually, I think I will invite him to our meetings…

During one of the MWMs we all noticed a couple of motorcycles drive by. One was a sport bike, or a crotch rocket, as I like to call them. The other one was a dual sport motorcycle that could go on or off road. We all stared at this bike as far as our necks would allow. Then, just after the bike got out of sight, Gary, one of the founders of MWM, said, "That would be so cool to have a bike like that and just ride all over the place." The MWM crew all responded with somber approval and excitement. Somber because everyone knew they would never buy a motorcycle or have the time to ride a motorcycle on some great adventure. Exciting because it was still fun to talk about it like it was a possibility. The conversation about riding the motorcycle continued for a while, and everyone was prophesying about where they would go and what they would do. Gary suggested going on a trip from New York to Fairbanks, Alaska and back again. Man, that would be so cool. Imagine what you would see. The deserts, mountains, valleys, and so much more. You would be totally free with the wind in your hair and bugs in your teeth. It would be a perfect trip. What a dream!!! A dream, POW, BANG, BOOM, SNAP, CRACKLE and POP. This was it. This is the dream that was going to turn me into a true ADVENTURER. I pronounced to the MWM: I am going to buy a motorcycle and head to Alaska. We all heard those words, but no one really believed.

The next day, while at work of course, I was looking online at all types of motorcycles. Suzuki, Harley Davidson, Yamaha, Kawasaki, and KTM. All of the bikes were so cool, but which one was I going to buy? I decided to head to Bob's Suzuki dealership in Pennsylvania. When I walked into the dealership, my heart was pounding. I asked myself, *Just what exactly do you think you are doing?* I walked around the showroom floor and saw a beautiful red V-STROM 650 dual sport. This motorcycle could go on and off road. THUMP, THUMP, THUMP. No, this was not an earthquake; it was my heart. I walked over to the clothing section and started looking at the riding gear. The coat fit perfectly. The pants, well they didn't fit perfectly, but I was able to get them around my belly. *What am I doing?!* I hung the riding gear back up on the rack and said to my wife, Joanne, "It is time to go." I started walking toward the door and could not get my eyes off the red Suzuki V-STROM.

"Excuse me, sir, sir?" I called for the salesperson. I

looked around and, not seeing anyone, I could only come to one conclusion. My subconscious mind was making my lips utter words I was too scared to say.

"How can I help you?"

I did not say a word at first, I just picked up my hand and pointed at the V-STROM. "Well, you made a good choice. That is the one motorcycle that will take you on any adventure that you want."

Adventure! OH SHIT! That was the perfect word.

"So, what are your plans, sir?"

"Well, I am thinking of taking a ride from New York to Fairbanks, Alaska and back again." *Did I just say that?! I did!!!* I was sweating up a storm. We went through all the features of the V-STROM, and it was perfect. So, what was the cost of the V-STROM? I was waiting for the price to destroy my adventurous expectations. The salesperson walked away and I took a couple more spins around the V-STROM, waiting for the price. I was awakened by the calls of the salesperson to come over to his desk. I pulled up a chair and sat down with anticipation.

"Well, today is your lucky day. That bike is on sale at cost. It's yours for $6,200."

I was blown away. I was expecting a price of $10,000 or more. A few minutes later the salesperson said, "Sign here, initial there, and the bike is yours." It felt like I had inhaled too much laughing gas as I picked up the pen, signed, and initialed the sales contract.

"Great doing business with you. Come back on Saturday to pick up the bike and take her home."

Did I just do what I think I did?

The following day at work, I heard the MWM roll call for our window meeting. There was a lot of chatter about the usual stuff as we stared out the window. A motorcycle drove by the window again, and some of the MWM'ers reiterated what we'd said at our previous MWM meeting.

"Guys, guys," I said, a little louder.

"What's up Patrick?"

"I purchased a motorcycle yesterday."

The room erupted.

"What kind of bike did you buy?"

"What do you plan on doing?"

"When do you pick it up?"

"Can I ride it?"

"Well, guys, we talked about taking a big trip, and I decided to jump right in. I plan on riding to Fairbanks, Alaska and back again."

"What the hell? That was my idea!" Gary chimed in halfheartedly. Everyone else was like, "Really?!" They were full of suggestions like "But you have to train for a ride like that," and "You should go out and take short trips and then work up to longer trip," and "The trip that you are planning is called an Iron Butt Ride, that takes endurance and you'll get big calluses on your butt."

"I need no training. You know what I say, 'Go Big, Go NOW, or Don't Go at All.'" They peppered me with questions like "Are you really going?" And "Wait, who are you going with?"

"I am going solo."

The MWM'ers sounded off, saying I was crazy. Well, maybe I was, but there is no reason that I need anyone else on this trip. I was taking an adventure. I felt so proud of myself for taking the challenge of doing something different and exciting. I had no idea what to expect, but that was part of the fun. The MWM'ers were all so impressed and excited.

The following day, my brother Gary and I drove to Bob's Cycle Shop and picked up the V-STROM 650. I did not have a license yet, but a permit should work provided I didn't get pulled over by a cop for doing something stupid. On the ride up, Gary and I talked about the trip, how long it would take, and my departure date. I was not sure of the specifics yet, but the departure date was going to be as soon as I could get all of the riding gear and saddle bags for the bike. I was hoping within a week or two. Upon arrival, the bike was brought out front. Gary and I were in amazement. The bike was just so cool. I slung my leg over the bike, and it felt so good. The plan of action was to have Gary follow right behind me to shield me from any potential police officers. It worked. I made it home without incident. On the way home, it was such a cool feeling to have the wind blowing into my helmet and wrapping around my body. It was a feeling of freedom and solitude. The solitude lasted for a few minutes until I start ripping down the highway at seventy miles per hour and got passed by a tractor trailer doing eighty miles per hour. You get blasted by the wind, and I mean blasted hard. What was also interesting was seeing the massive tires right beside me, humming on the pavement. The humming is loud, and all I could imagine was getting sucked under the truck and turned into a road pizza. I had a lot to learn.

The following day, I jumped online and ordered my riding pants, jacket, a new helmet, riding gloves, and three Givi saddle bags—one for each side, and one that would sit just behind the seat. The one behind the seat would prove to be a Godsend. More on that later. Once all of this was in order, the adventurer inside me grew, and I felt in a strange way distinct from what originally defined me as a person. Before, I was a mere mortal who did what was required of every person that wants to achieve the American dream. Work ten-hour days, be conservative, put all your extra cash into a savings account, mow the lawn, and most importantly, listen to your wife's demands and words of encouragement. Yeah right! Do this, do that, what you just did was wrong, I would have done it this way, etc. UGGGGH. What I dislike the most is when the wife says "Let's share a meal." I can honestly say that I have not had a full meal since the day I got married. I hate having someone rooting through my food before I eat it. The wife does this all the time, and before I get a chance to eat, I have a big mess on my plate. What a pain in the ass. The only person that I am willing to share a meal with is my youngest sister, Kori Princess Child.

I am not complaining about the life I currently have. I truly love my wife, Joanne. I have been blessed by a beautiful family, and truly blessed by God. I am not asking to change any of these things. I am merely looking to apply all of this love and support to other worldly adventures outside the bounds of mediocrity. As we all know, life is not limited to our surroundings. It is as big as the world, which contains endless adventures. To reach this world of adventure for the first time takes courage and no sense of reality, as we have no control over any of the events in our life anyway. So, take what control we do have by reaching out into the endless landscapes of our imagination and accept the consequences. Here is a saying that I created and now live by:

SUCCESS COMES FROM BIG DREAMS

A GREAT DEAL OF EFFORT

AND NO SENSE OF REALITY

(© 2006 written by Patrick Malyszek)

The meaning of this phrase, which I wrote while sitting at my desk at work, holds true for everything in life that you are willing to challenge. If you try to apply realistic expectations to everything you are trying to achieve, you will end up listening to the naysayers of life and melt into the socialized norms of inconsequential things. Don't forget, the easy answer to a challenge is always NO. Avoid this word like the plague. It is deadly. Always rely on yourself and what drives your heart and soul. Okay, enough preaching, let's get back to it.

With every twist of the wrench, I was gradually accepting the potential consequences of the adventure that is yet to come, but there was no fear, only anticipation. So, after a couple of hours in my garage, I grabbed the saddle bags and top case, and with a click they were attached to the motorcycle. I was almost ready to go. The only task left was to grab some tools, clothes and other essentials, put them into the cases, and then I'd be ready. I stepped back, looked at the V-STROM, and it looked pretty cool. I headed to the corner of the garage, closed the garage door, and before I turned off the lights, I took one final long look at the V-STROM. I went to bed with a great deal of satisfaction, as I knew that I had taken all the steps necessary to depart on my adventure. The final step would be to throw my leg over the V-STROM and head on out. It was only a matter of days until this glorious event would happen.

I went to the office the next day to get some work done to satisfy my clients and other obligations to ensure that upon my return I'd still have viable business. It was a stressful day, but a day of transition that was going to take me to the great beyond. With the ten hour day all wrapped up—one hour of which was spent viewing out the window with the MWM'ers—I was ready to make the transition. I could not wait to become that adventurer I always wanted to be. So, I left the office, went home, did a few final chores to ensure the horses would be well taken care of, looked at a couple of maps to assure myself that I was taking a reasonable route, and did a final gear check. I am sure that some of you thought, *A map?! Why not a GPS?* Well, a GPS was not part of the plan, and I wanted to follow my own path, not a computer-generated, pre-determined route that takes you through the most populated areas. I wanted everything to be my decision. I wanted real freedom. After all was said and done, I got ready for bed, and before laying my head down to sleep, I sat on the edge of the bed thinking about freedom, change in lifestyle, new beginnings, and the unknown. It was a very interesting couple of minutes that I hope everyone could one day experience. I gently placed my head on the pillow and closed my eyes. OOOHHH won't you know it, on this night I had so many dreams about this adventure and other adventures around the world—including hiking in the Alaskan outback solo. I guess what unlocked this door was the fact that I opened up my mind and my life to accept the proclivities of an adventurer who has only one fear in life. A fear of not being able to make the transition into the new Realm, which surrounds us all but only a few of us reach. This all sounds strange, but it is very real.

The rays of the morning sun eased their way into the bedroom, first hitting the floor, then the walls, the edge of the bed, and finally gently creeping up until the sun caressed my face and then my eyes. It felt so good to be awakened by the sun, like a hug of reassurance that there was another day of enlightenment yet to be experienced and another day of being loved. I swung my legs out of bed, got dressed, went back to feed the horses before my departure, giving them a little more feed and hay than usual, then headed back to the house. Once in the house, I took a quick shower, had a little to eat, and got dressed. This time, getting dressed was a little different. I was not putting on work clothes, I was putting on my riding gear. ALL RIGHT!!! All dressed and ready to go, I took a final walk through the house, turning everything off, locking a couple of doors, and then headed to the garage. I looked for my wife, but she had left for work early. I opened the garage door and there it was, all ready to go. I rolled the

V-STROM out into the driveway and shut the garage door. I turned toward the V-STROM, and it looked like a time travel machine. Every step I took now was a true transition into the world of an adventurer. Every step I took toward the V-STROM was thunderous and full of meaning. I grabbed the helmet, strapped it on, lifted up the face shield, put on my riding gloves, and did one final gear check to make sure that nothing would fall off. I swung my leg over the V-STROM and gazed around the yard, barn, and house. All appeared to be okay, but this was not an everything okay check. This was a check to see if there was anything that would hold me back check. There was nothing to hold me back. I grabbed the handlebars and with my foot firmly on the ground I hit the start button. The engine roared to life. I revved up the motor a couple of times and all sounded good. I pulled in the clutch and with my left foot I put the bike in gear. As I slowly let the clutch out and started moving forward, I knew the transition was complete as I rode down the street on what would end up being a 10,927-mile adventure. It was now a reality!!!

I hate to say it, but my first stop was at the office to wish my brothers goodbye. Gary and Wally met me at the front door and Brother Wally, whom I have a great deal of confidence in, did a bike check and made some adjustments to the suspension. This made a big difference in terms of managing the additional weight of the gear. Wally's most important contribution was tying a rosary to my handlebars so I would be safe on my travels. That rosary is still on the bike today and will remain there forever. Gary also did a full bike inspection, and everything looked good to go. You cannot forget that every adventurer has a great deal of support making everything possible from those that surround the adventurer with love. After a little more chit-chat, I jumped back on the V-STROM and headed west toward Buffalo, NY. One of the saddest things was knowing that I was leaving the MWM'ers and that Gary would be standing solo in the window wondering what his adventure would be. This was indeed sad. I knew that one day we would all do a ride together. I promised this to myself.

My trip to Buffalo, NY, was what I would call the White Knuckle Days (WKD), meaning that I was holding on to the handlebars so tightly that my knuckles turned white. At my first stop to put in gas, my hands were so stiff that it was hard to fully open them up. This was going to be fun for sure. Once the bike was filled with gas, I was back on the road riding through Elmira, NY, the soaring capital of the world. There was actually a person that took off in their glider from the Elmira Airport and flew all the way down to North Carolina without any engine power. That is a long way. What this translates to is that Elmira, NY is known for its windy conditions. I did not find this out until I was riding through Elmira on Route 17 West. I was happy as a clam in butter sauce traveling at about seventy miles per hour when a gust of wind hit me on my left-hand side. The gust was so strong that it pushed me sideways into the right-hand lane, my feet came off the foot pegs, and I had to lean like hell into the wind to keep from falling over. The bike was leaning so far that I actually had to take my right foot off the foot peg in order to regain my balance. If there had been a car in the other lane, I would have been road pizza. It was quite the rush, but it scared the hell out of me. I never expected the wind would be an issue, but it was for the entire trip. Sometimes the wind was natural, and other times I would get hit by the wind generated from cars and large trucks. I was dealing with the wind for the entire 10,927-mile trip. For the first couple of days, my neck was sore from fighting the wind gusts. It was truly interesting. By the time the trip was over, my neck was as thick as a tree trunk.

After I almost crashed from the wind, I decided to take a lunch break at Burger King. I needed to fill up my stomach after tossing my cookies from the near-crash, and to say a prayer or two. Okay, maybe like a couple of hundred prayers. After settling down, my grip on the handlebars was even worse. I also had to pay attention to the wind gusts, cars, trucks, and random animals crossing the road. There was a lot to think about in order to keep my butt in the saddle. I looked at my hands, and sure enough they were as white as freshly fallen snow. I just kept on thinking, *hold on, just hold on tight.* I thought if my neck was going to get thick, my forearms were going to get as big as watermelons, and they did. I was having fun!!! I would rather be holding onto motorcycle handlebars for my dear life than holding on to the arms of my office chair for dear life.

That reminded me of my time working for Lockheed Martin in Marietta, GA, as a contracts manager. It would get so boring due to the lack of work that I would challenge myself to see how many times I could spin in my office chair before I fell off or got sick. This contest went on for months, and each month I would increase the number of spins by a factor of ten. I never fell off the chair or got sick, but I did get dizzy a number of times to the point I could not read my computer screen. I was once asked by a coworker what I was doing. Being that I believe in the truth, I said "The boss wants me to put in overtime even though we have no work to do, so I've been working on perfecting the Office Chair Spin Games." My coworker just shook his head and walked away laughing. I am not sure if he was laughing at me or with me but either way, who cares? I was having fun. I did submit my office chair spin game to the Olympic committee for consideration, but they said no when they found out the development was funded by Lockheed and the government. Thus, it was government property. Boy, life is tough. I could have been somebody!

After a couple of hours of riding the back roads, I was

getting close to Buffalo, NY, which forced me to take the major highways through Buffalo and to the Canadian border. Upon reaching the Canadian border, I was asked to take off my helmet, show my passport, open my top case, and unzip my riding jacket. I was worried the next request was going to be "Drop your pants." That would have been ugly, being that I was going commando. After inspection, the border guard said be on your way. I proceeded for about a mile then pulled over to look at my map and my route to get around Lake Huron and back to Michigan. I had to take the QEW. The QEW is a Canadian highway where everyone on the eight-lane highway does about ninety miles per hour, bumper to bumper. It's a death trap for a motorcyclist. So, I gripped my handlebars even tighter as I felt like a small bug flying through a giant hailstorm, just waiting to get destroyed by a big chunk of cold steel. I had just started getting used to being the flying bug when, in an instant, traffic slowed and then stopped. I thought there was construction up ahead. That was not the case, as I started to see glass, bumpers, and other car parts lying all over the road. Someone had become the unfortunate flying bug that got tanked by some cold steel. I felt bad for them and said a prayer. So, with my grip now even tighter, I just held on and paid attention to everything around me. I only had another sixty miles and I would be off the QEW and traveling at a reasonable speed. I would no longer be the flying bug, rather I would be meals on wheels for the bears. Funny!!! Not really!!! I have been charged by a bear and it is not fun!!! More to come on that story.

Well, I did it. I made it off the QEW and finally hit the small backroads of Canada that were quiet, peaceful, and beautiful. I needed to relax after a long day, so I found a small hotel, checked in, and hit the mattress with a big sigh of relief. I wanted to get up and go to the bathroom, but the range of motion in my hands was not sufficient enough to perform the discrete cleaning operations. So, I had to wait, but I was safe. In about forty-five minutes, my hands had full feeling back, so I did what had to be done and went out to the vending machine to grab dinner: two bags of potato chips, a couple of cokes, and a few cookies. I was good to chase a couple of dreams. I was amazed with how sore I was after a full day of riding on the road. You would think that road riding is as easy as riding your lounge chair at home, but it is not. You are actually using quite a bit of muscle managing the bike and fighting the wind. If you plan on doing a motorcycle trip, I recommend getting off your lounge chair and getting in shape, fat boys and girls. Oh, one final tip for all the guys out there and maybe the girls, too, but the vibration of the motorcycles makes every tree, stone, and guardrail very attractive. Why, you ask? Well, the vibration makes you have to pee a lot. I never knew there was so much pee in me until I took this trip. I think I took a piss on every tree in Canada. I was respectful enough not to piss on any maple trees. You know the Canadian flag has a maple leaf in the center symbolizing hope, peace, and tranquility. My hope was to just go to the bathroom without being seen and to get some relief. Canada is true to its word!

The next morning, I got up, looked at my maps for the day, memorized my route, loaded the bike, grabbed some more chips, and I was back on the road. I mentioned being sore, but I failed to mention how sore my butt was from riding my first full day. OUCH!!! Every little squeeze, twitch, and adjustment was a little more than uncomfortable. The pain was even more special every time I swung my leg over the seat to get on the bike. Truly special indeed. My true concern was whether or not my butt would survive all of the days ahead. Time would tell. With my butt in the seat and a blue sky above, I started the bike, and I was off. The breeze from riding down the road was just amazing as it lapped around my body. It was like getting a massage. It was so relaxing. I was trying to figure out a way to get my butt in the air to take a bit of the breeze, but if I tried to ride the bike backward, I was sure I would have been mocked by onlookers, and I was sure that I would have crashed into the trees on the roadside. So, no butt massage today.

It was great being on the back roads where the frequency of cars was greatly reduced. There were so few vehicles that I was gradually starting to relax and enjoy all that was around me. My grip loosened, my white knuckles vanished, and nothing but joy filled my adventurous heart. I was relaxing into my trip and the unanticipated adventures yet to come. Well, this joyful heart was getting hungry, and I started looking for a place to grab lunch. One problem. I was in such remote country that restaurants were few and far between. After a couple of hours, I came around a corner and situated on the mountain top was a small little country restaurant. I cheered, hit the brakes, and pulled into the parking lot, which was quite full. I shut off my bike and took off my helmet and gloves. I left all of my black riding gear on because it was too much of a pain to take off and then put back on again. So, I walked into the restaurant and requested a table for one. The young lady who was a little put off by me said, "Please follow me." So, I did, dutifully. As I walked for what appeared to be forever, the waitress stopped and pointed at a lonely table in the corner and said, "There you go." I thought, *well this is out of the way, but so be it, I don't mind being alone.* What was interesting is how the patrons responded to a 6'3" biker dude wearing black riding gear and black boots that thundered every time they hit the floor. I felt like a bad-ass biker with everyone expecting me to demand free food—like I was going to start a fight and destroy the restaurant otherwise. I was laughing under my breath. The food was great and my waitress was actually very nice after she learned that I was not a scary biker dude but only someone out to have an adventure.

Just to maintain the image of biker dudes, I attempted to release right there in the restaurant what I had been holding for a long time, and that was a real big fart. Not a loud one but an SBD. You know—Silent, but Deadly! It backfired. Here was the problem of wearing riding gear that is waterproof. It means there is very little oxygen exchange from the outside air and the air trapped in your suit. Well, I got to the bike and unzipped my jacket and I got blasted with what would have sent the patrons on a stampede for the front door. I almost tossed my cookies. I am a mean one, and I got what I deserved. Never again will I try to fart in a restaurant with my riding gear on. It smelled so bad that I had to take off my riding suit and check for a little bit of blow by. If you do not know what that means you are probably a better person than I. So, with an all-clear assessment, I jumped back on the bike, hit the start button, pulled in the clutch, and with a gentle release I was back on the road getting the massage of my life. What is interesting is how the feel and vibration of the bike becomes part of you, and is with you for the rest of your life. If you don't understand, take a motorcycle adventure, or any adventure, and feel your psyche change as you are surrounded by your adventure forever.

One thing that I did not have on my trip was any type of radio to pass the time while on the road. Honestly, I really did not want a radio-equipped helmet, because I wanted the peace of my soul to guide my thoughts, many of which amazed me beyond my expectations. My thoughts during my traverse to Michigan were natural and unguided, and what came to mind were all of those who loved me. The amount of love I was feeling was like a blanket draped over me on a cold winter's night. A constant hug, a feeling of warmth, and a feeling of one hundred percent security that I knew would bless me during my travels, life, and well after that. I'd never felt love in this manner before, a love that reached out to me, a love that I did not have to earn. With this kind of love, one can never be alone. Some of the overwhelming thoughts were of my mother, father, and all the work they had done raising a family of eleven kids. They worked their asses off, giving all of us the best of their hearts and souls, along with great vacations. Great in the sense of family unity. We used to go to Walt Disney World every Easter. We did this for several years in a row, creating memories for the ages. The memories were not just of going on rides, eating too much popcorn, or watching the country bear jamboree a couple hundred times. What really stands out that made all of these trips special were all of the smiles and laughter that we generated as a family, with jokes, teasing, silly acts, and so many other crazy things. I remember the time when I was in the Magic Kingdom carrying my sister, Debby, on my shoulders. To my surprise I felt a rather large breeze on my butt. Sure enough, one of my brothers had grabbed my gym shorts and pulled them down to the ground. Having my sister on my shoulders meant I had to first put my sister down slowly and then grab my shorts and pull them back up. It only took a couple of seconds, but it felt like a lifetime. I was glad that I did not go commando on that day. It is thoughts like these that filled me with joy and happiness. If I'd had a radio, I would have missed these thoughts. On that day, my face was sore from smiling all day long at these memories. It was a great day, indeed.

With the day starting to wane I decided it was time to look for a place to stay for the night. I drove down a couple of dirt roads trying to find a place to camp. It was at this time that I found out the V-STROM had too much weight in the saddle bags and not enough upfront. This makes the front end of the bike very light, which means it can washout on corners easily. Translation: I could have easily crashed on dirt or wet roads with the bike in this condition. I almost did crash as I was rounding a corner. I turned the front wheel, and all it did was slide toward the trees. I have to be thankful that I was not going that fast, otherwise I would have left an imprint of my face on one of the trees. After almost crashing, I finally came to the end of the dirt road, and what was in front of me was Lake Superior. I walked out to the edge of the lake, thought about my family and loved ones, said a short prayer, then headed back down the dirt road to find a hotel. After an hour or so, I found a Days Inn, checked in, and relaxed for the night. It had been a truly amazing day.

The next morning, when I got up, I could still feel the vibration of the motorcycle and could not wait to get back on the bike again. After some eggs, bacon, and a few donuts, I was heading down the road again, getting that amazing massage. The plan for the day was to try and get back into the United States and hit Route 2 and take it all the way to Glacier National Park. One thing that was interesting about the trip so far was that in a lot of the remote places, I always found stacks of rocks. Sometimes they would be at the edge of the road, every couple of miles, but more often than not they'd be in remote places. Some of the stacked rock piles were fairly big and others small. I never really knew what these meant until I once asked a Native American, who told me the piles of rocks were basically sign markers to assist with spiritual navigation. The markers were left to recognize spirits of those that have gone before us and for those yet to join the spiritual world. I know that not all of the piles along the roadside carried spiritual significance, but those I found in the remote parts of my trip were old enough to be spiritual guideposts. I found this to be interesting, intriguing, and in a strange way, soothing. Soothing in the sense that we all know life is not endless and that at some point, all of us will transition into a new way of life.

The thoughts of transition are well hidden in our

subconscious mind, and for others it is a thought recognized frequently. My thoughts of the transition happen pretty close to daily. Not that I am living in fear, as I am not, but I think about what signposts or guideposts I am leaving behind every day. If someone were to follow the pile of rocks that I created, would they be led to spiritual salvation, or end up in the pits of hell? That is a tough call for sure, but I would truly hope that my path was guided by the stone piles of those that have gone before, and that I had an opportunity to make the path a little better and easier for others to follow. I don't know if I will ever get an answer to this question, but until I do, I will be listening to catch the spirits in the wind. I hope to catch spirits, and not bugs. You know, when riding a motorcycle, always keep your mouth closed. If you don't, your next meal just might be free.

Getting back to the acknowledged world—I was about three hours into my trip. With the crazy thoughts of rock piles and spirits well used up, I started drifting into singing songs to myself. The problem with this was I didn't know all of the words, so the songs ended up getting all messed up and lost in translation. I had a revelation! I would simply start my own personal radio station and call it "Patreeek FM." My radio station would only broadcast original songs. My own original songs, made up on the fly. The radio station was a great success and kept me entertained for the next thirty days of my trip. The songs were crazy, but it kept me laughing. I have a few of my songs recorded in writing but never would I sing them in the presence of any other person. NOPE! I can also honestly say that I have won several awards for my songs (in my head). One of the biggest is the CMT Award I got for singing a song entitled, "What Is a Butt Good for If You Can't Feel It?" I received best artist, best single, and best new country artist. I was a good day indeed!!!

After I was done accepting my CMT awards, I looked up and saw a sign that said *Michigan: 33 miles*. I was almost back in the United States. When I got to the border, there was a long line, but that was no surprise. As I waited, there was a car next to me with a little boy looking out the window, staring at me without pause. He was looking at the motorcycle, all of my gear, and then finally he asked, "What's on your wrist?"

"This?" I replied as I pointed to my right wrist.

"Yes," he said.

"That is my passport to get back into the United States."

The boy was just amazed. As we started to move forward, the boy said "You are so cool. I hope I can do what you are doing someday."

With moments to spare, I said, "One day, you will be an adventurer."

Was this a signpost, a pile of rocks that I'd just left

behind? I hope so, but I will never know. I will listen to my heart and say yes, I just left a pile of rocks to help guide that young boy to do adventurous things. I wonder if the boy ever bought a motorcycle and took an adventure. I hope so! Well, anyway, I pulled into the Canadian border checkpoint and the border guard appeared to be sick of his job and merely looked at my passport on my wrist and said "All was good." I let out the clutch and a few seconds later I was back in the United States and heading toward Wisconsin on Route 28. I finished up this day on the porch of a hotel watching the sunset, thinking about what a great day I had and hoping for more of the same tomorrow.

The following day, I was greeted with blue skies and a nice morning chill, a chill that would be considered warm once I hit the Yukon Territory. So, full anticipation, I packed my side and top cases, walked out to the motorcycle, and attached everything to the bike racks. With a flick of my thumb, the motorcycle came to life and I was back on the road. I was only a couple of days into the trip, and my passion for the road was growing exponentially with every mile. After about sixty miles or so, I saw a nice little restaurant and decided to have breakfast. I jumped off the bike and took my helmet off, leaving it on the bike this time. Again, the crowd openly moved out of my way, letting me by. They were all scared of this biker dude. This happened throughout the entire trip. I was getting used to it and found myself actually enjoying watching the patrons stare and move out of the way. It was another fantastic breakfast of eggs, sausage, and chocolate milk. Food of the gods! As I walked out of the restaurant, I was wondering if my helmet would still be hanging from the handlebars, and it was. If the helmet was stolen, I would be in a world of hurt until I found a new one.

I spent most of the day traveling through Wisconsin, enjoying the large farms and expanses of farmland. I have a small farm of seventy acres, which I own, and another three hundred acres that I lease for the purpose of making hay. During the spring, summer, and fall seasons, I am working almost nonstop to keep up with all of the chores, which does not include the time I spend at my offices providing consulting services. A typical day might consist of getting up an hour before sunrise, feeding the herd, repairing farm equipment, cutting the fields by 10:00 a.m., tending the field (which is spreading the hay out so it dries), and raking the fields I cut the day before. I spend the balance of the day making square and round hay bales. The square bales have to be hauled to the barn and stacked in the hay loft before the sun goes down, or before it rains. If square bales get wet, they are pretty much no good. More than a couple of times I have worked stacking hay in the loft until 2:00 a.m. It is a lot of work maintaining my small farm. I could only imagine the amount of work put in by the farmers in Wisconsin— and farmers in general. We should all stand up and applaud these hard workers that feed North America and beyond. I am now clapping wildly.

After taking some extra time to ride around some of these great farms, I realized that I was entering Minnesota. It was late, so I was now in search of a place to camp, or a hotel. I couldn't find any campsites, and I was not comfortable taking refuge on someone else's land for fear of getting shot. So, I holed up for the night in a hotel that was off the beaten path. It was a log-cabin style building with an amazing interior of wood, stuffed and mounted animals, and antique hunting equipment. After checking in, I took some time to take a short hike into the woods. I wanted to see some of the wildlife, hoping for a bear. After about an hour or so of searching, I decided to call it quits and head back to the room. Maybe I would see a bear tomorrow in my travels. Be careful what you wish for, as dreams do come true. The next morning, I was up early and ready to go find myself some food and hopefully get into the Dakotas before the day was out.

My primary route across the northern United States was Route 2, which takes you to Glacier National Park. Route 2 is a simple, two-lane road with very little traffic and a number of small towns, some in Native American territories, such as the Blackfeet Indian Reservation. What amazed me about Route 2 was the large number of crosses and stacks of rocks on the sides of the road. It seemed like there was either a cross or stack of rocks every couple of miles. I had never seen these crosses before, and later learned that each cross was the site of a car accident that took one life or more. When I learned this, I said a short prayer for all those that lost their lives in hopes of one day greeting these souls in the spirit world when my time comes. At a gas station, I was talking with a Native American woman, and she told me there was a very big drug problem in these areas. She said that sometimes people would intentionally speed down these roads with purposeful abandon, and others were influenced by the use of drugs, both resulting in untimely deaths. It was very shocking. The worst part of these deaths was thinking about the lack of self-worth these people felt before their recklessness took them to the spirit world. Just a little encouragement and confidence goes a long way to help people compel themselves to pursue a successful and meaningful life. I did not know how I could help, but I decided to always focus on the greatest qualities that each person I meet possesses and to encourage self-confidence. At my next stop, I told a waitress that she was doing a great job and that she should be given a raise. The smile on her face was out of this world. There was a lady in the restaurant that was nine months pregnant, and I could see that she was feeling miserable. I took the time to tell her that she looked absolutely beautiful. She reached out to give me hug and her face lit up with happiness. I do these things every day, and I hope my encouragement has a positive effect on those that I have met over the years. It is easy to be mean and negative, but it takes courage to be positive and happy. Challenge yourself to exude confidence and your life will change for the better. I promise!

Route 2 going through Minnesota and into North Dakota was a long, flat road that was very hot from the sun, with very few turns. My concern besides passing out from the heat was whether my tires were going to wear out and develop flat spots in the center. Yep, that is what had already started to happen. So, to minimize the growth of the flat spots on my tires, I decided to weave across the highway from shoulder to shoulder. I did this nonstop for hours, if not for most of the day. Did it help? Not really, but it was fun weaving. I made a game of it by seeing how many road lines I could weave through before I hit one. I got pretty good at it, but I was taking a risk of crashing, so I stopped playing the game. To pass the time, I turned on Patreeek FM radio and started composing more songs and singing. It was great fun, and I did not turn off Patreeek FM for most of the day. As I was singing, I noticed a lot of motorcycle riders going in all directions and realized that Sturgis, which is a large motorcycle gathering in South Dakota, had recently ended and that everyone was heading back to their regular life. What a bore! I felt bad for a leather-clad guy and his girlfriend, both of whom appeared to be frustrated. I walked over and complimented his nice bike to let him know I was friend and not foe. He talked about how much fun Sturgis was and about some of the wild activities. It really sounded like fun. I will do Sturgis someday. Anyway, he loved his Harley Davidson, but the gas tank was so small he had to stop at almost every gas station he saw. I asked him how far he had to go until he got home. California. Ouch! That is a long way to go on a two-gallon gas tank. I was going to suggest that he use a trailer next time, but I did not want to get my ass kicked. Well, I could have kicked his ass, but I think his girlfriend could have kicked mine. She was not fat at all, but she was in good shape. I was going to compliment her on being in shape in order to make her feel encouraged and confident, but there are certain times when a misspoken compliment will get your ass kicked. So, thinking clearly now—yes, I was thinking about what guys think of 2,656 times a day—I jumped back on the bike to continued my journey west.

Prior to becoming a motorcycle enthusiast, I noticed that every time motorcyclists passed each other they would always do a down-low wave by the engine. I thought this old tradition was a little stupid, but after I bought a bike, I followed the convention of all motorcyclists. Do a downlow, death-defying wave. Why? Just to be cool and fit in. Well, while I was traveling through South Dakota, I decided to defy this down-low convention and wave well above the gas tank.

So, I waited for my first victim. I saw a Harley Davidson rider coming toward me at a reasonably slow speed. So instead of doing the down-low, I did a full swinging wave over my head from right to left with great exaggeration. I mean my hand was really moving. I could see the face of the guy on the Harley Davidson, and I could see his head moving up and down. He was laughing at the fact that I was waving above the bike enthusiastically. By the time we passed each other, we were both laughing and smiling from ear to ear. From that day forward, I never did a down low wave again, and I still get the same reaction in most cases. Why be traditional when you have the option of generating a little bit of laughter? Even when I see my friends passing me, they all wave wildly over their head. I started a new trend. I call it "The Super Fun Wave."

With the Dakotas behind me, I was now traveling through the great state of Montana, flying along at a reasonable speed of seventy-five miles per hour. So far, my trip had blessed me with nothing but blue skies and warm days. This was starting to change. When I pulled over to stop for the night in Shelby, MN, the weather was perfect, so I went to a local steak house and ordered a full T-bone steak, a baked potato with everything, steak fries, and a ton of other good stuff. What made this meal special was the fact I did not get yelled at for ordering too much or ordering the most expensive meal on the menu. I also did not have to give my plate to the wife and let her rummage through my food for what she wanted first. I was able to totally relax and enjoy every bite. It was total heaven. What also made it special was the fact that the waitress was flirting with me the entire time. Not in a serious way, but in a happy and funny manner. I think that is why I ate so much food. We were having a great conversation and telling bad jokes. When I got back to the hotel, I decided to run five or six miles before I turned in for the night. The run was spectacular and a good change of pace from riding the motorcycle every day. So, from this point forward, I tried to run every night. Yeah right!!!

With a full belly from last night's dinner, I rolled out of bed the next morning with a sense of absolute freedom. One thing that I had not done on this trip at all was check the weather before departure. I really didn't see any sense in checking the weather, because it just did not matter. I was going riding regardless of what was thrown at me. Before I departed, I called my brother, Wally, to let him know where I was and that all was okay. Wally checked the weather for the morning in my area of the world and said to stay put for a couple of hours.

"Why?"

"There is a big storm heading your way."

"It cannot be that bad."

But Wally once again said to stay put. So, having a

great deal faith in Brother Wally, I stayed put and rode to the local motorcycle dealer to kill some time. When I walked out of the motorcycle shop, I noticed big, dark foreboding clouds rolling in. By the time I walked across the parking lot, it started to sprinkle. I put my helmet on and rushed back to the hotel. I pulled up to my hotel room door, brought the bike inside and then went out to see what the weather was doing. The rain had stopped, but the dark clouds still loomed with the threat of pouncing at any moment. While I was waiting, I saw a couple of motorcycles going down the highway. I asked myself if they were going to be in trouble. I did not know yet, but the clouds said run for cover. Wally was absolutely right on point. Not more than twenty minutes later, the skies opened up with a strong burst of wind that packed enough power to knock me off the bike had I been riding. A few minutes later came sheets of rain, and then hail the size of a penny. The hail was bouncing off the road like golf balls that had gone astray. The sound of the hail bouncing off the cars in the parking lot was as loud as a bad steel-drum rock band. If I was on the road traveling at seventy miles per hour, I would have had the poop beat out of me. Thinking it was over, I paused, but the wind speed picked up ten-fold and really started pushing everything over. There were garbage cans, wood, and tree branches flying and windows breaking. There was so much stuff going airborne that I thought about putting my helmet on, thinking a tornado was going to leap out of the dark foreboding clouds and take me away to the great land of OZ, just like Dorothy. Yep, a fool is defined by what a fool does and says. I did not put the helmet on.

When the storm passed, I had learned a great lesson: Always listen to my brother Wally. On this day, like others, he honestly saved my life. As I was getting back on the road again, I could see there was a great deal of debris on the roads. There were even a few cars with windshield damage. I was glad to have missed this storm, as I could have wound up as the debris on the road. I did pass the motorcyclists I saw before the storm, and they were held up under a bridge fixing their gear and drying out their clothes and helmets. I was glad they were okay. With the storm gone, I was able to relax back into the trip again but for the fact that the change in weather dropped the temperature by twenty degrees, which made riding a little chilly, but not uncomfortable. The uncomfortable chill would soon be defined as numb, freezing, shaking like a leaf, and the color purple. You cannot be scared of that which you have no knowledge, and I had no knowledge of what was yet to come. That is what I call a true adventurer. No plans, just grit and determination.

I was getting close to my right-hand turn into Canada and into Blackfeet Indian Reservation and Glacier National Park (GNP). My plan was to make it to GNP and find a hotel within the park to avoid camping, if possible, as I needed to shave and clean up a little. I looked like a dirty biker and probably smelled like one, too. I happened to pass the Many Glacier Hotel within GNP and decided to stay there. I pulled into the parking lot, and looking around, saw there was not a car to be seen. This was expected based upon the fact that I'd arrived after the height of the tourist season, and most people were thinking about getting back to school. I parked the bike, took off my helmet, and walked toward the hotel expecting to get a room, have a hot shower, and relax in a comfortable bed. When I walked into the lobby, the clerks behind the desk where shocked and stepped back from the counter as I approached. OOOOOHHH YEAAAAAH. I was wearing my motorcycle gear, my hair was a mess, and I had not had a shave in about a week or so. A badass dude I was not, but I must have looked scary. In an attempt to get the clerks to relax, I said, "As a weary traveler from New York, can I please have a room for the night?"

There was a long pause, the clerks looked at each other and actually said, "We are booked for the next several days."

Really? I did not see any cars in the parking lot. *Were they really booked?* I only needed a room for the night. The clerks, without even looking at the computer, said, "Fully booked."

"I am not a mean biker, I am just a weary traveler looking for a place to stay." The clerks restated their position from a little farther behind the counter. I did not want to push the issue, so I left and found a campground across the lake from the hotel. I did verify later on that night that the hotel had eighty percent of their rooms available. It is tough to be a biker. It appears the only way to be treated fairly is to be a badass. Geeeer!!!

I got to the campsite and set up my tent under a couple of bushes, started a small fire, and got ready for a good night's sleep on my 1.5-inch blowup mattress. Dinner was a bag of chips, soda, and some beef jerky. A short while after my camp was set up, a pick-up truck/camper pulled in a few campsites away. This was the only other person in the campground. Why in the hell camp next to someone? The worst predator in our humble world is our fellow human. I was concerned, and had my guard up for the unexpected. The driver, John, got out, set up a chair, and then meandered over to my campsite. We actually had a very nice conversation about the bear attacks in GNP over the last couple of days, the weather, and what to see in GNP. I was still on guard, but thinking that maybe John is not that much of a threat. During the course of conversation, the testosterone-based question always arises. I was asked what I do for a living. Okay, he is sizing me up, so I tell him I am a government contract consultant.

"How about you? What do you do for a source of income?"

He blew off my question and his demeanor changed drastically. I decided not to ask the question again, and the conversation transitioned to one of the most spectacular parts of GNP, the *Going to the Sun Road.* This road is carved out of the mountainside and lasts for miles. From various points, you can see small glaciers in the distance and just amazing views. If you decide to make a mistake while driving on this road, you will plunge to your death, as on one side you have the mountain as your guide and the other side your only guide is the deep blue sky. In other words, nothing but endless cliffs. When I was riding up this road, I made sure to look out for falling rocks that could knock me off the road, chicken-neckers, parked cars, and bears. At one point, I stopped and spotted a very small glacier, or should I say the remnants of what used to be a massive glacier that carved out the valley below and the mountain I was riding up. There was a time when the glaciers in this area were over five miles thick. Truly amazing!!! Just imagine the pressure and the power of this glacier and how it changed the landscapes and created the beautiful lakes that we admire today. Mother Nature never stops amazing me with her surprises. That is part of the reason why I love to do these types of trips, especially solo trips in Alaska. To be immersed in the natural beauty and the realm of the unknown takes you well beyond this world and into a world that is subject to no limitations and is filled with unlimited surprises, some of which let you know you are alive and others, if you survive, leave you feeling happy to still be alive. This is great stuff indeed!!!

Well, getting back to John. Like I said, his demeanor changed when I told him my work was related to the U.S. Government.

"So, have you traveled up Going to the Sun Road?"

John responded, "Not yet."

"I have not done it yet myself, but I heard it is amazing. I plan on doing it in the morning and then heading into Canada then up to Alaska. You should take that route and then drop back into the U.S."

John, without any form of hesitation, said, "No, I am not going to Canada. I am not crossing the border."

This was iterated more than once, and every time John was getting more restless. Something was out of sorts here. Something was definitely wrong. I got the feeling that John was on the lam from the law and did not want to do anything noticeable. A few minutes after this exchange, John abruptly stood up and walked back to his camper. As the day's light fluttered into darkness, I was concerned about the unknown moments of the night that stood before me. I had a few potential outcomes: John would kill me during the night, a bear would enter my tent, or it would be a quiet night without any problems. To secure my safety from John entering my tent, I pulled the zipper of my tent all the way to the top. For added security I grabbed a wire twist tie, the kind used on a bag holding a loaf of bread, and looped it through the zipper handle and wrapped the other end around a tent pole at the top of my tent. It felt like I was in Fort Knox. To protect against a bear attack, I merely said a few prayers and ate a small can of beans I had in my backpack. I should mention the consumption of beans was to generate some odoriferous fumes to let a bear know that what lay in the tent was nothing but old rotten meat. OHHHHHH!!! YES!!! SNIFF, SNIFF, it was working. I did not need a contingency plan for a quiet night. All was perfect in the world as I put my head down on my rolled-up riding coat. It was a good night's sleep until I was abruptly startled by the sound of an engine. It was John at about 5:00 a.m. He was pulling out of his campsite and continuing on his trip. I tried to get out of my tent to wave goodbye, but my twist tie security system worked amazingly well. It took me about ten minutes to figure out if I twisted the twist tie to the right or left. Stupid is as stupid does.

Once outside the tent, I extended my arms into the air over my head, I took a deep breath, arched my back, and reached for the rising sun. It felt good to be blessed with another day of adventure. On this day, I experienced all that Going to Sun Road had to offer, this being one of them, which I forever have recorded in the depth of my soul. "God does amazing things. Some that we recognize and others that are blurred by our desire to gain power and money. My choice as of this day was to recognize God's gifts every day and pass this joy to others." I hope I am judged by such things and not meaningless values placed upon all socialized humans. With this thought bouncing from ear to ear during the course of the day, I recognized that I was now approaching the Canadian border and headed toward Banff, Canada.

You know the definition of an adventurer, as I spoke about earlier, was really starting to change? It is amazing. I would attempt to explain, but I suggest at this moment for you, the reader, to become the adventurer and learn the true secrets of yourself and life, which is a lifelong quest.

As my travels continued beyond Going to the Sun Road, I saw a sign that said *Glacier National Parkway*. I said to myself, *I do not want to travel down a parkway*. The last thing I wanted to do was travel into a town full of stores and shopping centers. I hate shopping! So, I decided to take a left and head down an alternate road. I followed this beautiful road for hours. It took me through these narrow mountain roads, twisting and turning for miles. At one point, demolition workers were blasting along the road and I had to stop. As I was sitting there, I finally took a look at the map and realized that my impromptu left-hand turn had taken me west and not north. I'd made a big mistake. The Glacier National

Parkway was not a shopping parkway, rather it was a route that took you past a ton of glaciers. Thus, the Glacier National Parkway. Stupid is as stupid does.

The flag person saw that my head was down and he walked over to tap me on the shoulder with the butt end of his flag. "Let's go." Looking over the edge, I could see a small town in the valley below. Upon reaching the small eight-building town I got gas, checked my maps once again, and headed back in the direction I'd just come. The flag dude gave me a "what's up" gesture and with a chuckle and smile I waved enthusiastically, over my head of course, and enjoyed seeing the other side of the road I'd just traveled. I felt stupid for making such a dumb mistake. But mistakes are, in part, the essence of life, as they take you on unexpected journeys, some of which enhance your life with riches of excitement and others that make you want to poop your pants.

I finally got back to Glacier National Parkway heading north. This parkway was truly amazing, seeing the glaciers pouring into the valleys and how they'd carved the mountains into beautiful natural sculptures showing the timeless legacies of our world in each stone, cliff, and flowing river. As I was enjoying the silence offered by Mother Nature, I heard a sound. I looked up the mountain and could see a rock rolling down into the valley. It was obvious that Mother Nature was still defining her mountainous sculpture to meet the standards of her ever-changing beauty. The beauty in all things is never constant, rather beauty is defined differently every day, as every day brings changes to us as humans and the bounds of Mother Nature, which are unknown. Think for a minute outside yourself and imagine how much changes in our world every day. Hundreds of millions of changes every single day. Today is never the same as yesterday or the day yet to come. As we absorb this constant flux, we all must be open-minded, joyful, respectful, love those next to us, and help those who have lost their way. With these thoughts pounding through my head, I saw another rock chipped off the mountain sculpture. I looked to the right and saw a person standing there. I looked to my left, and noticed another person in view. I was supposed to love those who stand next to me. Well, the person to my right was an out of shape, sixty-year-old dude that had not taken a shower or a shaved in a while. The person to my left was a hot young lady that had probably worked out twice a day for the last thirty-two years. She was amazing. Can I be selective as to who I apply my newfound philosophy? If so, I pick the young lady who was very well sculpted by Mother Nature. At that very moment a huge rock came pounding off the mountain with a loud roar. It was heading for me. Okay, okay, okay. I chose to love them both. I reached over to give them both a kiss and…just kidding. It is important to love the spirits of those around us. A spirit that travels with the wind and speaks to us as it passes through the forests, valleys, and mountains. I made a veiled sign of the cross at both of them, said a simple prayer offering them the best life has to offer, and then turned toward my motorcycle to continue on my trip and listen to the spirits as I cut through the wind.

A little later in the day, after passing a ton of glaciers, I pulled into a rest area that allows you to walk on the glaciers after a short hike. I started up the path to the glacier and of course there was a crowd of mixed ages. In some places, I took the time to help those in need of assistance get over the gulches from the trail to the glacier. Once on the glacier, you get a feel for how big it currently is and can only imagine how big it must have been during the ice age and how cold it must have been here on Earth for these glaciers to grow so big and cover so much of North America. The real question is what caused the ice age. Do you know? What was really impressive was how the glacier appeared to be alive. There was so much activity, such as stones rolling down the glacier and water running on top of and under the glacier. You could see portions of the glacier that had collapsed and changed the course of the river. When you see pictures of glaciers in books and online, they appear to be motionless with no activity. This is not the case at all. They are very active, changing every second. These changes have been taking place for thousands of years and will continue well past the age of socialized humans.

There is a big push to save our glaciers and stop the inevitable and constant flux that comes with time. We have no control of time and the results that come as the result of time. It appears that even the most self-proclaimed experts feel they can alter the elements of time and forever stop Mother Nature's efforts to change and adapt. There is always that human need to be greater than that which surrounds you, and when that proves to be impossible, science makes up formulas, equations, and theories to cover up their ignorance. The world has taken care of itself for millions of years, and those that live in harmony survive, and those that refuse end up mutants. So, with all of this being said and to jump on the bandwagon, open up your freezer door every day for an hour so we can cool down the Earth and save our planet. Are you in? Ha ha.

After all of these wild thoughts and knowing that I have no control over Mother Nature, I stood up to take in the view once again then walked off the glacier and headed back to the parking lot. I threw my leg over the motorcycle and got ready to put my helmet on when I heard, "Hey! Hey! Meals on Wheels." I put my helmet back in my lap and looked around. I saw a guy walking in my direction. I said, "What's up?!"

With a British accent, he says, "I just wanted to talk to you about your motorcycle and your trip." The accent was great and made our conversation very enjoyable. He asked me all sorts of questions from how many miles I traveled in a day to what I have seen on my trip. I told him all the stories, and I think that he had vicariously taken my trip from New York to GNP. He turned, looked up the parking lot, and saw that his bus was loading up and started with his goodbye salutation. As he started walking away, I said, "Wait a minute, what does 'Meals on Wheels' mean?"

"It is simple. Those that ride motorcycle in bear country are ripe for the picking by a bear. So, Meals on Wheels. Just as another bus was pulling in, we saw a bear in the parking lot walking amongst the vehicles. Most people jumped in their cars for protection, but you have no car to jump into. That makes you an easy meal on wheels."

I was laughing my head off when he explained all of this to me, but he was right, I had no protection from a bear while on my motorcycle. As he got close to the bus, he said, "You are a true adventurer! Please be safe and have fun along the way." I was grateful to meet Giles from Britain. He was a charming lad.

With GNP now a memorable event it is time to focus on Banff, Canada. I had no real expectations of Banff but for the fact that I should be there after a short day's ride. As I was traveling, an old issue came up: How to stay warm on a motorcycle when it drops below fifty degrees. I had not solved this problem before, but the time had now come as the weather was reasonably cold every day now. I pulled off the remote road I was on, grabbed my map, and started looking for a motorcycle dealership that might have a heated vest. The closest one I found was in Calgary, about a two hour ride east of my location. I did not hesitate and took the enjoyable ride to Calgary. Once at the dealer, I grabbed the heated vest, attached it to my battery and hooked it up. It was sooooo nice to feel the heat of the vest. It made riding in the fifty degree weather extremely enjoyable but for the fact that my feet, hands, and legs were always cold.

With the heat of the vest warming me up, I rode back to Banff and proceeded to find a hotel for the night. I was truly amazed by the beauty of Banff and the surrounding area. The mountains were tall, the rivers and lakes were crystal clear, and the shops were all so very quaint. A perfect place to visit. I checked into the hotel, dropped off some of my gear, and headed into town to grab some food. When I was walking around town, the people were all very nice. It must be that Canadians have enough confidence not to be scared of bikers but to accept their adventurous souls and out-of-control looks. I grabbed some local food, some fudge, and soda for dinner then headed back to the hotel. It was all so comforting and very relaxing in this place called Banff. After eating dinner, I took a shower and dove into a bed with six pillows, all of which were lined up so very nicely. The blanket was soft and caressed me gently. I did not see the sun until the next morning. It was honestly close to one of the best night's sleep I've ever had in my life. I truly recommend going to Banff if you have time.

After struggling to get out of bed because it was so dang comfortable, I grabbed my gear, had a small breakfast, and could not wait to get back on the motorcycle again. You really do miss not being on the bike after a couple of hours. On this morning, I found another amazing gem, Lake Louise. This is a lake that was carved out of glaciers, some of which still exist to this day, with spectacular mountains surrounding three sides of the lake. I pulled into the parking lot, got off my bike, and spent a couple of hours walking around the lake and viewing the spectacular scenery. God has really blessed us with such great things. As I was enjoying the view I heard a ringing. Oh shit! I'd forgotten to turn off my cell phone. It was my brother, Gary, calling from my offices. "Pat, you just got a call from a guy that had his contract terminated for default and you need to call him back." I did not call this guy back immediately, so about one hour later Gary called me again demanding that I call him now. The mystery of my trip was shattered. I called the guy and gave him some direction, but decided I did not want him as a client at this time. He was upset, but I was not going to wreck my trip. After the call was over, I got off my stone perch nestled in a quiet corner by the lake and started to walk back toward my motorcycle. During this walk, I was thinking about my business, clients, work, billable time, and what bills had to be paid prior to my return. I definitely lost the flow of the trip and the spirits that carried me into another realm. I had to get back on track again. When I got to the bike, I grabbed my helmet, strapped it on tightly, zipped up my riding jacket, forced my fingers into my gloves, hit the start button, and let out the clutch slowly. I was back on the road again. The massage of the wind relaxed me, and the spirits of the wind started to whisper to me. After a short while the spirits surrounded me once again. I was back into my trip and enjoying the adventure. It is honestly hard to transition between our socialized world and the Realm that makes our lives special. The Realm is truly a great place, but it is ignored and lost to most.

My next stop was completely unknown, but Route 93N was just amazing. The mountains and valleys were all very impressive. What made all this even better was the fact that the roads were basically totally empty. It was relaxing. At one point during my travels on Route 93N, I was going through a series of valleys which had no trace of human existence but for the road I was on. When I started to travel out of the valley, I realized I was heading for a mountain pass. This pass was fairly high and full of twisting and very tight turns. A couple of the turns were so tight that I had to turn my handlebars as far as they would go to the right, and eventually the left. To do that on a motorcycle is extremely difficult. I wonder how cars made it around these tight corners. I stopped a couple of times to see if there were any car wrecks sitting on the side of the mountain. There was nothing, thank God!

When I got to the top of the pass, I pulled off the road and looked back from that which I just traveled. I could see the road for miles, with all of its twists and turns. It was a cool and transitional sight. It was like seeing the path of your life; all your trials and tribulations. Imagine, if you will, all the turns are challenging times while the straight portions of the road are the easy times of your life. If we mapped out our lives, I would imagine that we'd have more straight roads compared to challenging curves and turns. Life is better than all of our complaints. I thought about riding back down the mountain to do it again, but it was getting late, and I promised myself I would not ride in the dark nor attempt to repeat a life once lived.

On the other side of the pass, there was a sign reading *Jasper National Park*. That was going to be my destination for the day. When I arrived, I found a motel that was a little less than respectable, checked in, and looked for their vending machines to grab some food for dinner. The vending machine was full of bugs, so I decided to venture into the small town and grab some real food. The place I found was a local establishment in one of the nicer hotels. I was concerned about the quality of the food, but it was actually very good. I found a table outside on the patio and sat down to relax and enjoy the setting sun while eating dinner.

Not long after sitting down, four bikers walked over and joined me. We started talking about our adventures, destinations, and other random stories. It turned out that they were there for a family get together. The mother and father had their fully dressed Harleys, and their daughter and her boyfriend had Hondas. They started their trip from Montana and were headed up to Alaska. The parents were both retired and their daughter, Ashley, was a nurse. Ashley's boyfriend, if I recall, was an electrician. They of course asked me about what I do for a living and I told them that I am a government contract consultant working with companies all over the world and that I'd just finished working a big proposal for American Airlines. I explained that I was taking a break from work until the contract was awarded. It was a great conversation and after an hour or so I realized that Ashley's attention was focused on me, and she was asking me a lot of first-date kind of questions. I answered them all. We were laughing and having a great time. Every now and then I would look at her boyfriend and get the look of tolerance. I could only imagine him thinking that he would like to kill me, but there was no sense to him starting anything, as the night was getting late and things would end soon. He was right. So, one final set of drinks and it was time to call it a night. We all stood up and said our goodbyes and wished each other safe travels. Ashley asked me if I was staying at this hotel. I said I was staying at a place down the road, with my eyes as big as albino apples. I have never seen an albino apple, but...well, anyway you get the point. Her boyfriend was surprised by the question, and I was flattered for sure. She said, "Oh, that's too bad. Well can you meet us for breakfast tomorrow morning? My treat."

"I appreciate the invitation, but I am leaving early in the morning."

It was great meeting this family, but I thought I was going to get my ass kicked. After arriving back to the hotel safely, I hit the shower, cleaned some gear off, and hit the sack. It was a good night's sleep for sure.

The following morning, I woke up to a light rain. I took my time getting ready to depart by grabbing some food in the lobby. Before I entered the lobby area, I peeked around the corners to ensure there was no one there to kill me or buy me breakfast. I was safe. The rain had not stopped but it started to let up. The issue with riding in the rain is that you cannot see very well through your face shield, being that you have no automatic windshield wipers. Also, if you use your hand to wipe off the face shield it generally creates one big smudge spot that makes it even harder to see, and by the time you get your hand back on the handlebars, the face shield is coated with rain again. I have tried to use water resistant Rain-X that you apply to the shield, but that really doesn't work. For Rain-X to work you have to be traveling fairly fast to push the rain off. If you cannot see, you don't go fast.

Another issue with riding in the rain is that all of the dirt and small particles on the road float up, making the road surface very slippery. It's kind of like hydroplaning. Oil is another really big concern. You see, oil is normally very slippery, but when you add water it's like hitting a patch of ice in February with bald tires. Thus, when going around a corner, your front or back tire can slide out from under you and send you to the pavement. This also happens to be very painful as I have crashed in wet conditions in the past and it hurts badly. One time I crashed when I hit a patch of wet oil, and slid across the pavement, narrowly missing a steel guard rail. To this day I am grateful I did not hit those steel posts holding up the guard rail. If I had hit those posts, I would not be here today. One final note: When the roads are wet, the white and yellow lines and painted marks on the road offer no traction at all. So, if you are going around a corner and cross the yellow center line you will feel your front and back tire slide. Scary for sure!

Anyway, I ran back to get my gear and headed out. My plan of action was to continue west on Route 16 and find Route 37, which is a right-hand turn onto the Cassiar Highway. About twenty minutes after my departure, the rain started to pick up. My riding gear is waterproof, so I was not that concerned. Soon after I set off for the day, I saw Ashley and her boyfriend along the side of the road. I slowed down to determine if they'd crashed in the rain, but they were only putting on their rain gear. I honked the horn on my bike, gave a big over the head wave, and continued past them without stopping. I figured that if I stopped, I would have been left along the side the road dead by her boyfriend. Ashley waved. Amazingly enough, a couple hours later I decided to pull over into a tourist rest area that had gas, food, gifts shops, and much more. I went inside, grabbed some food, walked back to my motorcycle, and took a seat on the curb. I looked up across the parking lot and saw Ashley, her boyfriend, and her parents sitting at a picnic table. Ashley found me first, and she was staring and started to wave when her boyfriend put his arms around her and gave her a big kiss. He was jealous and was trying to gain her attention. He was also trying to prove a point to me. I did not want to instigate anything, so I stood up, waved for the final time, and relocated myself out of sight.

A few minutes after, I noticed a gentleman pulling into the parking lot and parking next to my bike. The type of bike he was riding was either a CZ or a Macio 250 that was made back in the 1980s. It had one cylinder, drum brakes on the back and front, and an old-style carburetor. In addition, he was wearing a white, old-style open-face helmet, with a Jaffa mouth guard, goggles, and an old leather coat that has seen more miles than the space shuttle. He had no saddle bags, only a backpack full of gear. What made this encounter even more fun was the fact this guy had a very strong accent. I asked where he hailed from, and he said Russia. Cool!

"So, what brings you to this part of the world?" I asked.

"Well, I am riding all around North America for the summer. I have ridden all over Europe, South America, Asia, etc...and wanted a change of view. I have been riding for years traveling the world. I have seen a lot."

"Have you used the same motorcycle for all of your adventures?" I was half-kidding when I asked this question, but he confirmed that he'd used the same motorcycle for all of these years. WOW!!! That is amazing. No GPS, cell phone, saddle bags, Garmin or inReach units. This guy was amazing and a true adventurer. With our conversation waning, I stood up, shook his hand goodbye, and wished him safe travels. I walked toward my motorcycle and took one final look in the direction of Ashley and her family, but they were nowhere to be found. I was safe to leave. The only thing that I regret about that day is that I never asked the guy from Russia for his contact information. It would have been cool to keep in touch. I will get it next time we meet for sure, in the event that we ever meet again.

I still had a lot of miles to cover before I had to start looking for Route 37. With a couple of hours under my belt, I checked my map and realized that I was not going to make it before nightfall, so I started looking for a place to stay. As I was riding along in this part of the world, I noticed the foliage had changed drastically. Were the leaves falling off? No, because most of the trees were pines. I took a closer look and saw that a majority of the pine trees were dead. I wondered why. Well, I soon learned of a beetle infestation that burrows into the trees and kills them. This was a big problem for this area. I would like to know how this area looks today. I wonder? Well, anyway, during my search for a place to stay I noticed there was a big drop in temperature, and I was getting cold. Just as the sun was setting, I found a little mom & pop motel and was happy to get my boots off to relax. There was no TV in the room, or any type of radio, so I made it a quick night and just went straight to bed. The following morning, I grabbed my stuff and headed for my bike. I noticed that it was cold but did not realize how cold it really was until I reached my bike. There was frost all over it. It was below freezing. Wow! Below freezing in late August. I was surprised. I scraped off the seat, gas tank, and the windshield. With the weather so cold, I had to worry about the potential of ice on the roads. I hit the start button, plugged in my heated vest, and I was off. My chest was as cold as frozen peas. After some time traveling, the temperature picked up into the fifties and the sun came out. So, all was good with the world, and I was warming up.

I looked up and there it was, a small sign reading

Route 37. I blinked and missed the turn. When I actually got on Route 37, I stopped and said, "Is this really it?" The road was narrow with over-hanging trees and more dirt than pavement. I continued for another couple of miles and saw another sign. I was on the Cassiar Highway. Holy remote. There was nothing. So, without anticipation, I continued. One thing that I did notice was the sound I heard between my legs was getting louder. I stopped and pulled over. I looked at the cases for a crack, the frame, and I started the bike to listen but could not locate the sound. I thought the clutch might be breaking or maybe there was an issue with a cycler. Without having an answer, the only answer was to keep on going until something really broke. So, I started the bike, listened, and there was no miracle; the sound was still there.

So, frustrated and worried about finding a place to fix the bike if it did break, it weighed heavily on my mind. As I was riding along, I started to test the bike by going faster and faster. I hit around eighty-five miles per hour on back country dirt roads. What a fool!!! If I had crashed on this road, no one would have found me for months, if at all. I was being stupid. I slowed down and started to enjoy the trip again. If it breaks, it breaks. During my travels on this dirt road, I started to come down a section into a valley with trees hanging over the road so densely that the light of sun was blocked out. It was so dark and creepy. As I was rounding a long, right-hand turn, I was surprised to see a big log cabin surrounded by helicopters, at least four. I decided to pull in and see what was up and get some food if they had any available. This place was a heli-skiing port during the winter that took skiers up to the mountain peaks. It was such a cool place. I can close my eyes now and see every detail. One such detail was they had one old gas pump surrounded by two stone columns with a roof. This gas pump was not capable of taking credit cards, and there were no buttons to select the grade of gas you wanted. You only had one choice: regular. The place was called Bell 2 Lodge. If you like to ski and enjoy cabins and being outdoors, this is the place to go. Within the lodge, there was a small restaurant in which I was the only patron. The hostess and I found a table; I sat down and hung out for few until someone came over.

"Nice to see you again." The hostess was also the waitress.

I said, "What is good in this joint?"

"Well," the waitress said, "it is not a matter of what is good, it is a matter of what we have to offer."

"Okay! So, what do you have to offer?"

"Well, see that dumpster outside?"

"Well, yes."

"If you dig in the back left corner you might find some meat the bears left behind last night."

"Is it cooked?" I asked. We both started laughing. With a big smile on her face she said, "I can get you a burger with some fries."

"Really?! That would be perfect."

A little while later, she brought out a simmering burger and hot fries smothered in salt. It really hit the spot. With the check in hand, I walked over to the register to pay for my food, and she was there again.

"So, you are the hostess, waitress, and cashier. Who does the cooking?"

"I do!"

"Wow! You are amazing, because you do everything perfectly. They should give you a big raise."

"Yeah right!" She was thankful for the compliment, and I was thankful for the few laughs that we had.

"Have a great one!" I said and headed outside to continue on my adventure.

My destination for the night was going to be Dease Lake. I was hoping there would be a place to stay. When I entered the town, it was quaint and isolated with not very many features. It was basically a nice homesteading town with one gas station. The local bar and restaurant were closed, but food was readily available at the gas station. With so much being closed, I was happy to find a hotel with a room. Being it was so late in the season, the hotel was wide open. As the night closed out the day, it started to rain. I was hoping it would rain out during the night, which it did, but everything was still wet in the morning. With not too much to worry about, I searched for the strange sound that had been haunting me. After a few minutes of searching again, I grabbed my engine guards. Sure enough, where they connect in front of the bike, I found a crack in the mount. The mount was vibrating, making the scary noise. I was happy the problem was only superficial and not serious.

As I threw my leg over the bike, it started to rain, but there was no reason to wait. As I was heading down the highway, there was a bit of an uphill, then a downhill left-hand turn and an immediate right. The road was wet and muddy. As I took the downhill left, I kept to the inside— not all the way, but across the midpoint line of the road. I looked up and saw my first car in a day and half. The car was in the center of the road as was I. I turned the handlebars to the right; the front tires started plowing the mud, and my momentum was taking me right at the car. I immediately thought that I needed rudders. I took my feet off the foot pegs of the bike and put them both on the road in the mud. I used my feet to steer by alternating the pressure on each leg. My first act was to avoid a head-on collision. I put pressure on my right leg and the bike started to move right. Holy shit, this might work. The car was trying to slow down, but its tires were locked up and skidding. We were both panicked. He was worried about denting his car and I was concerned about breaking my leg. I put more pressure on my right leg. I could now feel rocks rolling under my feet. More pressure, Scotty! I literally put all of my pressure on my right leg by standing up on it. I started pulling on the handlebars with all of my might. Time was starting to slow down, and everything went into slow motion.

I was *pulling, pulling, pulling.* The bike started to slide slowly to the right. It was working, but not fast enough. I turned the handlebars all the way to the right. My butt was off the seat as I was putting more pressure on my right foot. I saw the front bumper of the car, took a big breath, closed my eyes, and hoped that my riding gear would not be polishing the bumper of the car. Here was the bumper. No pain. I looked up and saw the rear-view mirror coming at me. No pain, I looked inside the window and all I saw was the big, bulging eyes of the person driving the car. No pain. I saw the rear bumper, which lightly brushed against my leg, but still no pain. The car disappeared.

Wait, I expected pain. Nothing!!! I looked up, and there was nothing in front of me but open, muddy road. Holy POOP! There was no bone-breaking contact. There was no bump. There was scraping. There were no guttural sounds of breaking bones. I'd made it!!! I was still in one piece. I was so happy that I stopped paying attention to the road and drove into a large tree. Just kidding. I was very happy that I missed the car. I would have hated to end my trip in a hospital.

With the threat of hitting the only car I saw that day now behind me, I relaxed, and decided my destination for the night would be Watson Lake, the location of the renowned Sign Post Forest. Back in the 1940s, when the Alaska Highway was being built, construction workers started to post signs. Today there are more than 86,000 signs in this one location. The signs have names, messages, locations, and other wild stuff. I have my sign hanging up there, and it simply reads "Patreeek." It is hard to see in this picture, but it's just down this path to the right.

As I was pulling into Watson Lake, it was about two hours before sunset. So, I hung my sign, walked through town, and decided to find a campground for the night.

What was amazing is how empty it was and how much of the town was closed. I was there in September, and pretty much all of the tourists were gone for the season. I walked into a local bar that was occupied by four people and asked if there was a campground that I could stay at for the night. The bartender said about ten miles out of town you will find one. As I headed for the door, the bartender said that they'd been having trouble with bears. The game warden, who was one of the four people in the bar, said they'd almost had one captured, but it got away and it was injured. Well, that was great news. I would be careful.

I headed toward the campground and in a few minutes saw the sign that said, *Campground this way*. I started down the dirt road, and there was absolutely nothing. No buildings, no campsites, no nothing. I traveled for about two miles and finally I saw some campsites, but still no buildings. What was more interesting was the fact that there was absolutely no one in the campground at all. Not a soul. I looked for a suitable spot that was flat, unloaded my bike, set up the tent, and then traveled back to the bar to get some food. I ordered a steak and ate every bit of it along with the potatoes. It was a great, filling meal. I later learned that my steak was not beef but moose. It was very good. After eating, I flew back up to my campsite, parked the bike and just relaxed. My main concern about being so off the road was that someone could come into the campground and kill me and take all of my stuff without anyone knowing. My second concern was the wounded bear.

A couple hours later I was sitting next to my tent, and sure enough I heard a four-wheeler coming down the road into the campground. Wait a minute! It was well after dark. There was no one else in the campground but me, so why was this person coming into camp at this time of night? My first concern was coming true. I quickly turned off my flashlight and moved my bike behind a couple of trees to avoid reflections from the person's lights. I just sat and waited to see what was going to happen. I followed the light on the four-wheeler moving slowly around the campsites. What was this person looking for? Why were they moving so slowly? I did not know, and I did not want to expose myself, fearing that this person had bad intensions. There was a chance, however, that it was someone from the bar trying to warn me about the bear, but that was unlikely. I could not take the chance.

All of a sudden, I saw lights coming across the forest headed in my direction. Oh, shit! I hit the dirt! As the lights were getting closer, I was planning my next move, which was to run for my tent and grab some type of weapon. Well, I had no real weapon, so I grabbed a heavy stick that was lying at my feet, ran back behind a couple of trees to hide, and just waited. The light never made it to me or my tent. The person on the four-wheeler turned around and headed back down toward the main drag. All this took about forty-five minutes, which seemed like hours. Okay, enough adventure for one night. Time to go to bed. I climbed into the tent, jumped into the sleeping bag, and zipped it up. I was ready for a good night's sleep.

Then it hit. My eyes popped open. I grabbed for the zipper, but I could not find it at first. ZIPPPPPPP went the sleeping bag and ZIPPPP went the tent. I was free. Okay, which way do I go? I looked around and saw nothing. Nothing at all. Okay! What did I see when I was coming into camp? Think man, think. Oh yes, it was over in the other campsite, about five hundred feet away. It was time to get rid of the moose meat. Moose meat is good going in and rough going out. As I started to head to the wooden latrine, I heard a large crack in the woods. What the hell was that? I walked a few more steps, and I heard more cracking and the sound of brush moving. Oh, come on! I am being followed, and it is too dark to figure out what it was. I had to go, badly, so I continued my approach to the wooden, broken-down latrine. I was almost there. Thank God!

I got in, grabbed for the button on my pants and pulled the pants down as fast as possible, squirting along the way. Yes, it was a bad one. With great relief I settled into the wooden seat and waited until all was cleared. Then I heard the cracking sound again, again, and again.

It was getting closer. The cracks turned into shuffles. It sounded big. I reached for the small hook and latched it through the hole. This took a few tries, as I could not see very much in the dark. I'd left the flashlight in my tent. I did not feel safe at all. I was trying to decide what to do when there was another blow by of moose meat. Okay, so running at this point was out of the question. As I was sitting there trying to figure out what to do, I was thinking what the news line would be back home. *Man in the Yukon Killed by Bear While Taking a Shit!* Embarrassing or what?! Despite my concern, I was laughing my head off at the potential headlines. Laughing so hard that I cleared the last bits of moose meat. With everything cleared and cleaned—I think—I decided to head back to my tent. So, I opened the door very slowly, listened, and heard nothing. I stopped and listened about every ten steps and made it back to the tent without hearing a sound in the woods. I did not want to get back into my tent immediately, so I took a seat against a pine tree about fifteen feet away and listened. I heard nothing for about fifteen minutes. Life is good. Then there was a big ruckus in the woods. My friend was back. I stood up slowly, looked in the direction of the sound and could not see what was so interested in me. I did hear heavy snorting. I was being tested, and, like in school, I failed. I reached for my helmet strapped it on, heard some more snorting, jumped on the bike, hit the start button and headed back to the bar to see if they had a room available for the night.

I was so concerned for my life that I left everything behind.

When I walked into the bar, it was about 11:30 p.m. and there were now five people sitting there drinking and consorting. I asked the bartender if he had a room available for the night. He said sure, but why? Well, I was at the campground and there was something in the woods stalking me. It followed me to the latrine and into my camp.

"Yep! That's about right!" he said.

"What?!"

"That is where we last saw the wounded bear. You are lucky that you were not attacked!"

Well, thanks for telling me, I said to myself. As I was walking up to the room, I could hear the guys at the bar laughing. Despite the humiliation, I crashed for the night in a dump of a room, but it did have four walls, a ceiling, and floor for protection. No bears here!

The next morning, I got up and headed back to camp to get all of the gear that I'd left behind. Sure enough, I found bear tracks around my tent. I'd gotten lucky. What was more amazing was the fact that my sixth sense was spot on in terms of the person on the four-wheeler and seeing a bear. I have learned to rely heavily on my sixth sense, and it has saved my butt several times on my other Alaskan adventures. My sixth sense was now telling me to move on up the road and find new adventures. So, I did.

On this day I had no real plans or expectations. I just wanted to ride and enjoy the wind cutting through my helmet and my spirit being lifted by the majesty of all that was around me. I was in heaven. As I was motoring along, I saw amazing mountains, rivers, and forests that went on forever. Imagine, if you will, the amount of life that exists within a forest that appears so calm and inviting. There are millions of creatures and animals all fighting for survival the same way we are all looking to make money. It is unreal. If you think about it, our daily lives take us away from the natural world and leave us in our small cocoons of a home, car, and office space.

We spend most of our time hidden away from nature and complain when Mother Nature does not give us what society deems as perfect weather. Mother Nature gives us a world exactly how it should be with rain, snow, seasons, and storms. Without these things, the world would not exist as we know it today. Nearly everything that we build, manufacture, or change is to push Mother Nature away from us. For example, we as humans try to build all forms of sustainable energy, such as, nuclear plants, electric power stations, and electric storage devices to make life easier for us all. If you really think about it, Mother Nature has created a sustainable self-producing energy source that has existed for millions of years. That source of energy is nature itself. To go beyond nature is a recipe for disaster. The easier life gets, the more technology is needed to maintain the easier life. It is a dangerous cycle indeed that will one day yield to an environmental reset of all things. It has happened before and it will happen again. I just hope the reset of the world doesn't happen until I have had a good dinner with some chocolate chips cookies for dessert. The bottom line is that life is what it is going to be, so love life like you have never before and have a chocolate chip cookie to end every blessed day.

With the crazy thoughts of Mother Nature waning, I decided to grab the final chocolate chip cookie in my backpack. I sat on the dirt road, leaned against the stone next to my bike, and slowly ate the cookie. It was absolutely fantastic. I can still feel the joy and the taste of that cookie today. It was truly mesmerizing. With a sugar high in full swing, I jumped back on the bike to continue on my way. What was yet to come was unknown, and I looked forward to meeting it.

As I was buzzing along, I had an opportunity to see some buffalo. Not in the fields, but right in the middle of the road. I attempted to ride around them, but they kept moving toward me. I did not want to get chased, so I back pedaled for about a hundred feet and sat and just waited. It was cool to see the wild buffalo. They are *big* animals. With the buffalo now dispersed, I was able to create a plume of dust as I traveled down the road. With the plume of dust growing as I picked up speed, it started to drizzle. Not very hard, but enough to wet down the road. No more dust clouds.

As I came into a valley, I could see a very large river flowing at a rapid pace. I watched and saw a bridge in the distance and without any real concern I maintained my speed of about sixty miles per hour. Upon my entry onto the bridge, I realized the decking of the bridge was made up of uneven wooden planks. Wet wooden planks!!! Oh shit. You see, wet wood planks are very slippery. Kind of like riding on ice. I immediately felt the front end sliding all over the place. I wanted to hit the brakes, but that would have been deadly. So, I backed off the throttle. This helped, but on more the one occasion my rear tire started sliding and I would head for the wooden guardrail. The guardrail was just high enough to stop my bike from going over, but not me. I was waiting to do a flip off the bridge into the raging river. I did hit the guardrail once, but at a very slow speed so there was just a small bump and a gentle fart of relief. I burned another one of my nine lives. This stuff was scary, but I am a real adrenaline junky. So, the high I get is a compelling driver to just keep on going. I wonder how many people said they were adrenaline junkies and ended up cold, surrounded by soft white cushions, and a pine box. Probably one too many.

Once I was off the bridge, I pulled over to check out my maps, which were telling me that my next destination would be Destruction Bay. Prior to getting there, the road looped around and between the mountain on the left and the lake to the right. It appeared that this portion of the road had experienced some landslides, and there was a construction crew working on clearing and fixing the road. The equipment they were using were very large earth-moving dump trucks, such as Moxy Rock Trucks and large excavators. When I pulled into the construction area, I was flagged down to a stop. I pulled up to the flag person and to my surprise, it was a beautiful young lady with a hell of a tan. I never would have expected to see such a girl out in the middle of nowhere working a construction job. We had time to talk because one of the large Moxy Rock Trucks was stuck in the mud. So, during the wait, we got talking about the area and other fun stuff.

It was a great conversation, but once the Moxy was pulled out, she hit me on the back and said, "Time to go." I said thanks, pulled in the clutch, and I was off. As I was driving by the other equipment and workers, I noticed the entire crew was all young ladies and everyone was a real knockout. It goes to show you that beauty can move mountains.

It was not very long until I arrived in a small town with a hotel, restaurant, gas station, and boat launch.

With my arrival in Destruction Bay, the population was literally doubled. It was me and the local resident who owned and operated the entire town. I asked if there was a room available. He said, "Well, buddy, being that no one else is here or in town and it is late in the year, I have plenty of rooms available."

I checked in and went to my room with a mattress and a box spring. It was not much, but it was all good. Once I got settled, I went back to the restaurant, grabbed a table by the window overlooking the lake, and actually had a real nice dinner. I woke up the next morning to cold weather, overcast skies, and rain. I thought about staying in Destruction Bay for the day, but I missed not being on the bike. I was excited to go.

As the day continued, the weather got worse, and the rain continued at a fairly hard pace. I had confidence in my waterproof riding gear and had no concerns about getting wet. What was a pain was the fact that I could not keep my face shield clear of the water droplets and the occasional mud. I kept on trying to wipe it clean and dry it off but that only made things worse. After a while, I got used to not being able to see and decided to keep on riding with a wet face shield. What else could possibly get wet? Well, I noticed that my gloves were starting to get wet, and the rain was creeping up my arms and down into the gloves. This was not a real problem but for the fact that the rain was cold and it was only about forty-five degrees. My hands were starting to get cold, and I had to keep on taking my hands, one hand at a time, off the handlebars in order to wiggle my fingers and try to regain some warmth. It felt good to move my fingers, but it really did nothing for getting my hands warm again. Being a real trooper, I continued on my journey without any real concerns about the continued rainfall. I did pull over at one point to plug in my heated vest, as I was starting to get a real chill. It helped for sure. A little farther down the road the clouds darkened, and rain started coming down like a lumberjack sliding down a greased power pole, fast and hard. I am not sure why a lumberjack would even climb a greased power pole, but the analogy works, right? Well, anyway, I was going to pull over but there was no real place to hide on these remote, back country roads, so I continued.

I accepted the fact that I had wet hands, it was only forty-five degrees, raining, chilly, and that I could not see clearly out of my face shield. It was all part of the fun. Despite these few irritating issues, the mountains were spectacular. Just looking up and seeing the challenges they have to offer is amazing. Imagine, if you will, living in a small cabin and waking up every day to the challenge of survival, the solitude of your own soul, and nothing but silence. Cool, or what?! This is the life I would love to live. I actually had a plan to leave for Alaska and find my place of silence and solitude. I was very close to departing forever, but my favorite puppy dog, named

Yukon, would have missed me too much. Yukon has since passed on, so I am trying to reignite this dream. It was so much fun playing with Yukon, as every time we played outside and went hunting, I would think of the bear that charged me on one of my Alaska trips. You see, I was kneeling at the foot of my tent…drip…drip…drip. *What the hell is that?!!!* Okay, great, the rain had found a way through the zipper of my riding pants. This was now getting uncomfortable. I had water dripping into my nether regions, running down my right leg into my boot. It felt like I had pissed my pants. OOOOOOOOHHHHHH now it is running down my other leg. Is there no shame? This SUCKS!!! I remembered what wet diapers felt like. But it was not over yet.

The rain began hitting my neck and running onto my chest. It found the connection to my heated vest and the warmth I so enjoyed faded quickly. I was totally soaked at this point and getting very cold. I was freezing. I needed to find a place to stop for the night, but there was no place close. I continued on for a couple more hours. During this time, I was hoping the rain would stop, and at one moment it did, and I was extremely hopeful that I would soon warm up. OH GOD is good! OHHHHHH NO! I think that I pissed off God, or maybe God was honoring my wish and expectations. You see, the rain did actually stop, but within a few minutes it started to snoooooow…I needed to be a little more specific about what I was asking for when I asked God for the rain to stop. I would try again. *Dear God, can I please have you move the clouds so the sun can shine through?* I waited as snow was now sticking to my face shield, the backs of my hands, everywhere. My butt was cold. God did not answer my prayer this time, at least not as I intended, so I kept on moving forward hoping that good things were on the way.

As I traveled forward, I had to navigate a couple of tight corners by slowing down to a crawl. I reached for the clutch lever and my fingers would not move. I backed off the throttle to buy more time before I had to take the first corner. To my surprise, my throttle hand would only open up just enough to allow the throttle body to slide back, reducing the speed of the bike. I had a pair of hard-ons, as both hands were stiff as frozen cucumbers left outside during the month of February. I made it around the corners, but it was extremely difficult working the controls. I had to find a dry place to pull over for the night.

After a few more long but joyful hours, I coined myself *Frosty the Snowman on Wheels*. Everything was cold, stiff, and covered with a thin layer of ice. I finally reached a town located on the Yukon River. It was White Horse. My first course of business was to find a place to stay that would provide warmth, shelter, and protection from the elements. It was a Days Inn. I pulled into the parking lot, left all my gear on the bike, and headed for the registration desk where I was greeted by nice young lady.

I blurted out with no semblance of control, "I would like a room please."

I sounded desperate, because I was. I was shaking from the cold and the lady asked if I would like to dance? What?! She was making fun of the fact that I was shaking so much.

She said, "I need you to fill this out and sign at the bottom. Oh, and by the way, I also need your credit card."

Not a problem. I took my riding gloves off and for the first time noticed that my fingers were actually deep blue. I was shocked. I attempted to pick up the pen she gave me, and I could not close my fingers on the pen. The young lady was laughing at me as I was laughing at myself.

"Can I just give you my credit card for now, if I can get into my wallet, and complete this form later?"

"Sure," she said.

So, after dropping my wallet on the floor a couple of times, I finally was able to get it on the counter. I actually gave her my wallet and she took out the credit card for me. In a very nice and sweet voice she asked why was I on a motorcycle this time of year, as it was September.

"Well, I am traveling up to Fairbanks and then back

to New York."

"What?! You are traveling north to Alaska? What are you, stupid? Motorcyclists are out of this part of the North Country by now. We had a couple inches of snow on the ground this time last year."

I had no defense to her comments. As I was shaking, my hands were blue, and I encountered snow and some ice, I realized she was absolutely right. I smiled with a puppyish expression of stupidity hoping to hide my ignorance. I don't think it worked.

She merely said, "Your room is to your left and the best of luck in your travels, especially since you are still heading north."

Yep, she thought that I was stupid.

When I got to the room, I stripped off all of my wet clothes, jumped into bed, and piled on all of the blankets, pillows, towels, and a few cushions. It took me hours to stop shivering. At one point, I turned on the shower as hot as it would go, got in, and stood there in painful gratitude until the hot water ran out. When I got out of the shower I walked by the mirror, screamed—in a manly kind of way, of course ha ha—and said, "What is that?"

I took two steps back, looked square in the mirror, and there was the largest lobster I had ever seen. Yep! The hot water was a little too hot, and it had irritated every portion of my body. Like a sunburn. I was waiting for the pain but luckily enough there was no pain to be had. I am glad that no one knew this part of the story until now. Prior to this disclosure, sometimes I would hear people making general comments using the phrase "Big Red." I would immediately stop to see if they were talking about me. I was just being paranoid, but I was personally embarrassed every time.

I skipped dinner and hit the sack early. I planned on getting up a little early in order to avoid the lady at the front desk that had checked me in. I knew if I saw her, she would give me hell for still traveling north. When I was ready to leave the room, I looked out the window and saw blue skies. The forecast was showing temperatures in the sixties with a little chance of rain. God answered my prayers, but just a little late.

It was time to go. Like a spy on a covert mission, I opened the bedroom door very slowly, put my face to the door and peered out the two inches of open space. I saw no one in the hallway and opened the door just wide enough to slide out. Once in the hallway, I tiptoed toward the elevator, listening closely for any sound of footsteps. Nothing! *I am doing good!* I hit the down button, heard a sound and started tiptoeing back toward the room as fast as I could. With my heart in my throat, I reached for my room key. OHHHH fudge cakes! I'd left the key in the room. I paused. Wait! The sound I heard was the elevator coming to pick me up. Dumb Ass! I tiptoed it, at high speed, to catch the elevator. I just barely made it. You know, it is so very hard to tiptoe in motorcycle boots. I wonder just how dumb I looked. Well, anyway, the hard part of the spy game was yet to come. When the elevator doors opened, I would be in range of the front desk. I needed to be stealthy like the wolf. The doors started to open, and my heart was pounding. Before the doors opened fully, I was out tiptoeing it to the pillar. I made it without being seen. I looked at the front desk and there was no one. Was this my chance to make it past the hotel clerk? By the way, her name was Jessica. From my concealed position, I looked at my path from the pillar to the front door. It all looked good. On the count of five, I was going for it. Five, four, three, two, one, and I was off. There was no one. I only had a few more feet to get past the front desk. I made it. With no other place to hide. I was going for the front door. The door opened automatically. I'd made it.

"Patrick, Patrick, oh, Patrick!" I stiffened up and quietly said, "Oh, shit."

"Would you like your receipt?" It was Jessica.

"Sure, I would like a receipt."

"You look a lot better today than last night. What time did the dance end?"

Laughing, I said, "Well, I stopped shaking around 2:30 in the morning. Should I fill out the registration now?"

"No. It is not really needed. I hope you have safe travels today. The weather is excellent to the south."

Ouch. Another friendly dig.

"Which way are you going today?"

"Honestly, I am still heading north. I want to complete my trip by making it to Fairbanks, Alaska. I am so close now."

She laughed in a very kind way and said, "Well, have a great rest of your trip. I will be thinking of you."

"Greatly appreciated." I headed out the door with a large smile on my face. What a beautiful way to start the day.

On this leg of the trip, I was to cross into Alaska. I was close to my destination of Fairbanks and would be there in a few days. On this day there was no real challenge, so I made up a new game. This game was called jumper. The roads in Alaska are subject to extreme cold, which causes the roads to heave up, and during the summer the heaves do not go away completely, so you have jumps. The first time I hit one of these frost heaves I was shocked, as the bike bounced hard. So, whenever I saw a heave in the road, I would turn it into a jump by lifting the front end and then cracking on the throttle. This would allow me to get some airtime. My goal was to see how far I could fly. I never flew very far, but it was fun trying. At one point I hit a real big one, got some good airtime, but bottomed out the back end on the tire. This was a hard hit. I then decided to stop jumping the frost heaves as I was concerned about crashing and breaking the bike. When this fun came to an end, I saw a sign that said *Welcome to Alaska*. I made it! I was so excited. The first half of my trip was almost over.

When I got to Fairbanks, my plan was to meet up with my favorite cousin, Mark Malyszek, who'd traveled with my brother Wally to attend Fairbanks University. My brother Wally had come home after graduation, but Mark had decided to stay in Alaska and work at the school for the next thirty years. Actually, Mark just recently retired, got married, and now lives in Virginia. What made Mark my favorite cousin is the fact that every time I see him, he is full of life, joy, and good jokes. Well, not all of his jokes are good, but either way they made for a good laugh. Mark's laughter has had a true impression on my entire life, along with my father, mother, and all of my brothers, sisters, cousins, aunts, and uncles.

When I arrived at Mark's place, he was gracious enough to give me a room to stay in at his apartment. We went out to dinner at one of the finer spots in Alaska, we caught a movie, and actually saw the northern lights as we were walking back to his apartment. Mark also took me on a tour of the Museum of the North, which gives a very cool history of Alaskan Natives, prehistoric animals, and a lot of other interesting stuff.

The next morning, Mark made some eggs, sausage, and toast for breakfast. I wanted to stay longer, but I had to hit the road to start the second half of the trip, which was getting back home. I jumped on the bike started it, and Mark said, "Let's do a vehicle check." So, we checked all of the turn signals, brake lights, the headlight, and the front and back brakes. This was a simple check, but it was a memorable moment because all Malyszeks are selfless and we always take care of each other. Well, kinda!

Before I officially left Alaska, I took some time to see what Alaska had to offer. I found this old gold dredge, which is a massive machine used to gather gold in the middle of nowhere, surrounded by trees and mountains. What was strange was that the dredge was floating in a small body of water. Okay, so how does this thing move and gather gold? Simple!!! See, you first dig a pond about one acre in size, let it fill with water, and then you actually build the gold dredge so it floats in the center of the pond. In front of the dredge there is a long-extended boom with a bunch of inverted buckets that rotates. As it rotates the buckets digs into the earth and the dirt is deposited within the dredge and processed to find gold. As the dredge digs, it creates a channel in front which allows the dredge to move forward. As it moves forward, the excess dirt is deposited behind the dredge. It is a very cool system that was developed back in the 1900s. There are gold miners today that are still using some of these old dredges in Alaska. If you would like to see one, watch the show called *Gold Rush* on the Discovery Channel.

After seeing the gold dredge, I wanted to try my hand at finding some gold and found a place that would allow me to do some gold panning. I grabbed a gold pan, walked over to the creek, and started panning for gold. After my first attempt there was nothing in the pan. I kept on trying for a couple of hours, and still nothing at all. It was getting late, so I decided to try one more pan. I finally found a couple of flakes of gold. I felt proud of the fact that I found some gold, but found out that when I took a break to hit the bathroom, the owner of the property put some gold in my pan. I was actually grateful because the excitement of finding some gold was a lot of fun. The next time I go gold mining I am going to buy a large excavator, dump trucks, and a gold processing plant. Well, as soon as I have an extra $2.5 million on hand. With the morning pretty much expended, I had to hit the road.

On my way home, I decided to stay in Canada all the way back to the New York border. I took the Trans Canadian Highway. The trip home for the most part was fairly simple, thank God, as I was on paved roads most of the way. When I got around Lake Superior, I decided to take random back-country roads. This was a lot of fun, as there were no expectations at all in terms of where I would end up and what I might see. I remember riding down Route 129, which led into 17. Without looking at a map, I took the next route I saw. As I was riding down this rural route, I ended up seeing a big black bear on the side of the road. I was concerned the bear might run into the road, so I took a very wide swing into the other lane. To see a bear is to see freedom, adventure, and the spirit of our souls.

A little farther down the road, I was playing games by chasing birds that landed on the road. This was fun, as I knew I would never really be able to catch or even scare a bird. At least this was what I thought. At one point, I did see a bird sitting in the center of the road. So, I accelerated and headed straight for the bird. I was getting closer, closer, closer. The bird never really seemed interested in moving. So, I started to slow down, then started moving out of the way when the bird took off and flew into the side of my boot. The poor bird was shredded by my boot and motorcycle. There was no saving it. I was very disappointed in myself for playing this game. I never thought in a million years that I would have hit the bird. Stupid is as stupid does.

My random selection of routes ended up putting me on Route 6. This remote route took me past some very nice countryside. At one point, I saw signs that said *Ferry*

Boat. Really? I continued on, and I ended up in a small town called South Baymouth. To continue on to Route 6 I had to take a ferry (Owen Sound Transportation South) to cross Georgian Bay to Tobermony. The departure time for the next ferry was a couple of hours away. As I waited, there was no one around, but as time passed the loading area filled up. When the time came, I pulled my bike into the belly of the ferry, tied it down, and headed to the upper deck.

What was very impressive was that this ferry boat had a fully loaded logging truck on board. I was honestly concerned about the boat sinking as another fifty cars were loaded. When I got to the upper deck, all I wanted to do was find a quiet area of the boat and just relax. No human interaction. I wanted nothing to do with anyone else. I contributed this feeling to the fact that I had been alone for such a long time now that I was enjoying my silence and solitude. Wouldn't you know it, as I was walking back to my yet-discovered remote area of the boat, I saw a group of bikers. One of the bikers asked how my trip was going and I said just fine.

"Yeah, we just did a big 300-mile loop around the lakes. Man, it was a big trip. Where are you coming from?"

"Well, I'm doing a round trip from New York to Alaska and now I am heading home to New York."

"Really? WOW! What a great trip! That is amazing."

I went from just another biker to celebrity status in a matter of seconds.

"Oh, man! Tell us about your trip."

"Well, it was fun and challenging."

This group of bikers followed me around for the entire ferry ride across the Georgian Bay. If I walked, they walked. If I went to the bathroom, they would. It was like this for most of the trip. I could not get a break. Toward the end of the ferry ride, I finally got away and had a chance to relax. I was hiding in the lower deck with my bike. I truly appreciated their interest, but I just wanted to hang by myself.

When I got off the ferry, I finally looked at the map and decided to head to Hamilton, Canada for the night. It was getting late, so I had to travel with some haste as I do not like to travel at night. About an hour after leaving the confines of the ferry, it started to rain. It ended up raining all the way to Hamilton. With the rain and the clouds, nightfall came early, and I found myself riding in the rain in the dark. A dangerous proposition for sure. I did promise myself that I would never ride at night, because it was way too dangerous, but on this night, I was wet, cold, and wanted to reach Hamilton, which put me in range to reach home the next day. Being that it was dark and raining, it was very hard to keep my face shield clean enough to comfortably see the road. I kept on wiping my face shield but that only made things worse.

Despite that fact that I could not see very well, I continued to fight the elements. I was almost there. I wiped my face shield again and with only seconds of clarity I saw something crossing the road. I wiped again and sure enough, it was a raccoon or an opossum. It was in my way. I had to move, but there was no time. I just held my breath, slowed down, and watched my front tire miss the animal within an inch. Man, I almost died. If I'd hit this poor animal, it would have kicked out my front tire, and I would have hit the road and cracked open like an egg before it goes into the frying pan. *Okay*, I said to myself, *time to find a place to stay for the night*. I stopped at the first hotel, and I got the biker look and response.

"I am sorry, but there are no rooms available in this area, they are all booked."

"Really?! Why?"

"Well, they just are. You will need to travel to the next county, which is another sixty miles down the road."

I walked back out into the rain, jumped on the bike, and started moving down the road. I got about two miles down the road and decided the hotel clerk was full of poop. I stopped at the next hotel.

"Are there any rooms available?"

"Why, yes. We are not even close to full."

"Really! I stopped at the hotel just up the road and they said I had to travel to the next county to find a room."

"They lied to you. There are plenty of rooms available, being the travel season ended a couple weeks ago."

The look of a biker had done it again. Well, I was glad to get into the room and dry off. It was a long day on the road and the rain had made it even more uncomfortable.

The next day, I crossed into Buffalo, NY and headed toward Route 22 East, then Route 17. When I hit Buffalo, the realization of my trip coming to an end, after being on the road for a month, was very depressing. I'd grown to love being on the road and enjoying the sights, sounds, and just being alone. It was going to be hard to be home again. I made this last leg of the trip last as long as possible by throttling back to about forty miles an hour. I wanted the trip to last forever. I know that nothing lasts forever, but I prolonged the trip by a couple of hours. The one thing that does last forever are the memories. A day never goes by without a thought of the trip, the fun I had, and the great people I met along the way. The best memory, as strange as this might sound, is the memory of myself. You see, on all of my adventures I am usually going solo. When you are alone, you have a chance to become your independent self, free from socialized influences that train you to be proper, socially responsible, and to hide your weaknesses from others. You never really learn who you are. When you are alone in the wilderness or taking an adventure alone, you have no choice but to learn who you are; adapt or die. So, as I sit writing this paragraph, I am lost, because I know who I am, and that is the person I left behind when the trip ended. I will find myself again by taking more solo trips.

Story 2

Crashed and Broken

Every year, I take a trip to remote parts of Alaska that are only accessible by float planes. Most of my trips are generally done solo, but in some cases, when I am lazy, I will hire a guide service. The best guide service in Alaska is Alaska Alpine Adventures (AAA). They offer a lot of great adventures and happened to have a trip that takes you through the Neacola Mountains, located in Lake Clark National Preserve. This is a trip that I have always wanted to do and planned on doing solo. My wife, however, secretly went behind my back and set me up to go with AAA on this particular trip. I understood her reasoning, being that I have no life insurance. She did not want to lose half of her domesticated income. Just kidding. I guess. Well, anyway, the Neacola Mountains are vast, steep, and offer very little room for mistakes. I know this because I have attempted this trip on three separate occasions and failed every time. One of my failures almost took my life, and the other time I was unable to eat any food for twelve days. Mortality is real.

I found this out when I crashed and broke myself in Alaska during these trips. I will pay for these crashes for the rest of my life.

Death Avoided

Prior to the beginning of this trip, I trained very hard for twelve months lifting weights, running mile after mile with a seventy-pound weighted vest, cross training in extremely cold temperatures, and getting used to being cold, wet, and miserable. It was hard work, but the intent of this training was to get in shape and get comfortable with being uncomfortable all the time. Did it work? Well, no matter how hard you train, there is no such thing as a comfortable or a pain-free trip. The key to success is having the ability to accept hours of painful physical exertion, coupled with mental courage to fight like hell to reach your destination, or survive the worst possible outcome. I was ready. At least I thought I was ready.

On a day in August, I was to meet my guide and two other adventurous souls in Port Alsworth, Alaska. As I waited, I grabbed all of my gear, dumped it on the bank of Lake Clark, and decided to do another gear check. Yep. I had my knife, some extra emergency food (Hershey Bars), a full bottle of water, tent, Garmin inReach unit—which is a GPS tracker that has a save-my-butt button, sleeping bag, and extra clothes in order to stay dry in the event of an emergency. Most of this gear was packed into dry sacks to protect it from getting wet and to ensure that I had something dry at my disposal. To get wet in Alaska and not have dry clothes could result in hypothermia in a short period of time.

As I was repacking my backpack, I heard a plane landing at Port Alsworth. It was the guide, plus the two other adventurers. We all sat on the bank of the lake, introduced ourselves, and talked about the trip yet to come as the guide passed out lunch bags with potato chips, sodas, and peanut butter and jelly sandwiches. A few minutes after eating our lunch, our guide, Andy, took the time to talk about the dangers of bear encounters, our twelve-day schedule, glacier travel, and river crossings. It was a very informative meeting, but nothing goes as planned, and we should have been planning for the unknown. I know it is hard to plan for the unknown, but it is possible if you plan for the worst, having no other expectations. We failed miserably at planning for the unknown on this trip. We all paid for it dearly with pain, discomfort, hypothermia, blood, and a twenty-four-hour rescue mission.

It was time to board the float plane to the middle of nowhere. We grabbed our gear, walked toward the plane, and started to stuff our packs into the back of the plane behind the seats. There was no particular order, we just kept on stuffing. Once all of the gear was loaded, it was time for all of us to pile into the Cessna 206. The pilot told me to take the co-pilot seat. I think this was because I was a little taller and bigger than the others. I also think he was trying to distribute the weight to make it easier to take off.

Prior to take off, the pilot went through the same procedure as stewardesses do on a large plane.

"Please buckle your seat belts by pulling on this clasp and inserting the flat silver side into the buckle. In the event of a plane crash, you have two exits. One to the left of the pilot and the other one is also on your left side. It is the door that you used to load the plane."

In other words, the only way to get out was to your left.

"To open the door just lift the silver handle and either push outward or pull the door back. It depends on where you are sitting."

Great instructions. Which one is it? What was interesting is there were no doors, at least on this plane, on the right side. So, if there was a crash, and I was the only survivor, I would have to crawl out of my seat and over the pilot or anyone else piled against the doors before the plane sank or caught fire. This did not give me a sense of confidence at all. In these small planes, it really does not matter, because if you crash, there is not much of a chance of getting out alive, unless you are in real good standing with God.

With the FAA comments rightfully expressed, the bush pilot turned his attention to the dashboard of the plane. I analyzed his every move because I knew from watching movies that I might have to take control of the plane and successfully land it back at Port Alsworth. I would be the hero…Right! Anyway, as I watched his sequence, I noticed a couple of times he would reach in front of me and adjust a couple of knobs. There was so little space that my left knee was hitting the knobs. I am not sure, but I think one was used to control the fuel mixture and the other one was for prop control. I did not really know, but all I wanted to do was keep away from these knobs. The pilot hit the start switch and the engine roared to life.

The pilot, by swinging his hand, caught my attention and pointed at something on my right-hand side. I turned the palms of my hands up, gesturing *What's up?!* He reached across me and grabbed the headset and gestured for me to put it on. The engine was running, and I could not hear a thing. When I put them on, the sound of the engine was bearable and relaxing.

"Hey Patrick… Patrick." *Who said that?* Oh my gosh, was that God talking to me? Was God trying to give me a warning? Holy poop, I better say my prayers. What a dumb ass! It was the pilot talking to me through the headset.

"What's up?!"

The pilot told me to keep my knees off those knobs.

"Not a problem." I said.

With a few more twists of the knobs, the engine of the plane grew stronger and we started to pick up speed as we crossed the bay. At the end of the bay was a large mountain. We were heading straight for it. I was not very concerned, but we maintained the same elevation heading directly toward the mountain for a few more minutes before we took off and headed north. Our destination was Turquoise Lake, the entry point into the Neacola Mountains.

With my head leaning against the cockpit window, I was entranced by the mountains, valleys, and waterfalls outside. We passed over some of the mountains and others we flew right next to. We were so close that I thought I could have reached out and touched them. It was so cool and transformative. At one point, we spotted a bear running along the mountainside. It looked big from the plane. I could only imagine how big the bear really was. The pilot and I were trying to find out what it was chasing but did not have the time. I was so focused on the bear and the landscape that I did not notice that my knee actually hit one of the knobs pretty hard. The pilot immediately hit my leg and said, "Pay attention. I do not want to crash out here in the middle of nowhere." From that point on I did not hit any of the knobs again. To crash in this remote area would definitely change the course of the trip, if not end it for all of us permanently.

As we crested one of the mountains, the pilot said, "There it is, Turquoise Lake." We took a descending, hard right-hand turn and started heading up the lake at about 300 feet above the surface of the water. On the far side of the lake there were massive mountains on both sides. In the middle was a big river flowing out of the mountains with multiple tributaries from smaller canyons high up in the mountain ranges. It was freaking cool. As we approached the end of the lake, I was trying to figure out how we planned on turning the plane around to make a landing. We started to gain elevation. I looked down and the water of the lake turned into nothing but gravel. What was going on? We flew deeper into the valley of the two mountains, gained a little more elevation, then turned toward the mountain on the right. It was getting closer, closer, and closer. I started to hum the Lord's Prayer. *Is this going to hurt?* I wondered. *Wait, was my knee hitting the knobs causing us to fly into the mountains?* At this point in the flight, I had to piss so bad that to let my knees drift apart would have been very embarrassing. I checked my knees anyway and they were clinched together so tight that it hurt, but I needed to create a little more resistance against what was trying to escape.

"Hey, Patrick what is going on over there?"

"What do you mean?"

"You are humming what I believe to be the Lord's Prayer. Are you?"

"I am just fine but I do have a question. Is there a point in time when we take a left turn away from the mountain in front of us?"

"Oh, yes, we should have turned a little sooner, but here we go."

We did a full turn to the left and within moments we had the lake back in front of us. I am truly amazed by the fact that we had a ton of room to turn the plane.

"See, Patrick, we had plenty of space to turn the plane. You better now?"

"Yep!!! I was never really concerned or scared. NOPE! Not this tough guy."

The pilot did not buy it at all.

We finally landed on the lake, turned toward the headwaters, and beached the plane on the right side of the river. The first thing I did was find a bush to release the pressure. It felt sooooo good. By the time I got back to the plane, the guys had most of the gear out and lying on the shore. Once all of the gear was removed, the pilot jumped in the plane and headed back to Port Alsworth. Watching the plane taxi down the lake and take off is always a sobering feeling. I suggest that everyone experience this feeling at least once in their life. The feeling of being left alone in the middle of nowhere.

Andy, our guide, wanted to have one last meeting before we headed up the river basin. We discussed the importance of being smart, not taking any chances or making any dynamic moves when walking on treacherous terrain. Before Andy wrapped up our meeting, I asked for everyone's attention, the purpose of which was to let the group know that I had a satellite phone, and a Garmin inReach unit in addition to what Andy brought with him. I did a brief orientation on how to use the Garmin and initiate a rescue beacon in the event that anyone was injured. The one thing that I learned from doing a lot of these trips is that redundancies can save your life. A prime example is having a set a of matches and flint to start fires. The matches stay in your backpack and the flint is usually in your pants pocket, or better yet, hanging around your neck. I keep mine around my neck so if I am ever separated from my backpack, I have a means of starting a fire. Fire is life!

With the final checks complete, we heaved our backpacks on our backs and started up the valley. The river valley was mostly washed cobblestones, boulders, mud, and a little vegetation. In other words, this was great hiking because it was flat and there was no fighting the alders or other brush. Alders are shrub type plant that grow at the lower elevations in Alaska and are thick and intertwined to the point that they are very hard to walk through. Alders are no fun at all and require a great amount of mental and physical strength. The only thing that really got in the way of having a straightforward first day of hiking was the river that meandered back and forth across the valley. Every time we had to cross meant taking off your boots, socks, and rolling up your pants, which never stayed up and always got wet. At one point, the river was too deep to cross, so we navigated up a real steep cliff that took us to fifty feet above the river and carefully worked our way around using the small ledges and small trees to keep from falling backward.

This traverse was about 500 feet long. It was hard work, being that you had to face the cliff at all times and balance the weight of the backpack that was constantly pulling you backward. When you are in this kind of situation, you are using every muscle in your body. It hurts!!! The other side of the equation is your mental toughness. You need to have confidence without limits, as Alaska is limitless and if you blink when doing these types of activities it could spell disaster. When making this crossing, I made the mistake of looking down between my legs. I saw the raging river full of rapids moving as fast as spaghetti covered in tomato sauce sliding off your fork just before putting it in your mouth. I looked up as fast as I could and concentrated on not falling into the river. I was back on the move when I placed my foot on an unstable rock, and sure enough, my right foot came off the cliff. I reached for the ledge above me, grabbed it with both hands, and held on until I found a better foot placement. I thought I was going to bounce down the cliff into the river, but my conditioning and mental fortitude is what made the difference. I concentrated hard on the task at hand to complete the last 200 feet. I was very cautious and tested every foot placement before applying my full weight. I made it! This was not as scary as it sounds, but any form of injury can be costly if you are not within reaching distance of civilization.

By the time we made it back down to the river basin, the clouds darkened and it started to rain pretty hard. We donned our raincoats and continued our journey into the mountains of Mordor, as I like to call them. Both sides of the river had massive 2,000-foot cliffs as black as night. It was dark due to the conditions and the height of the cliffs, which blocked what available light there was. It was very eerie, with the mist of the clouds the sounds of the river, and the falling rocks. I bet this is what Frodo experienced in the *Lord of the Rings*. It was foreboding and soon to become formidable.

The goal for the day was to make it to the end of the valley and set up camp on the tongue of the glacier. The only problems with this plan were the unknown conditions and the obstacles encountered earlier in the day that took more time than expected. What made matters even worse was the amount of rain. It rained, and rained hard, to the point where the drops had a bit of sting to them when you got hit. It was tough going, but we really needed to get to the glacier, otherwise the trip schedule would be all screwed up. Andy was getting nervous and wanted to go. So, we persevered. As we continued, small tributaries that had not been there before started to appear and grow. I looked up at the towering cliffs, and there were now a ton of waterfalls flowing into the river basin from the right and left sides of the canyon. I wondered just how big the plateau was at the top of the cliffs. They must have been massive to create the size of these waterfalls.

With all of this water, the river started to rise to the point that it could not be forded by merely walking across it. In order to get on the tongue of the glacier and start the next part of the journey, we had to cross to the left side of the river, then climb onto the glacier and follow it to the top of the mountain. With the river so high, and getting higher by the minute, the decision was made by Commander Andy, to find a spot to camp for the night.

"Guys, we will be staying here for the night. The river is too high for a crossing. We will wait out the rain, let the river levels drop during the night and try to find a spot to cross tomorrow."

It was nice to stop for the night, set up the tents, and get my warm sleeping bag ready. Once my tent was set up, I helped Andy set up the cook tent. We had fairly good food to keep our bodies generating some heat. Food is critical to keeping warm.

The night brought nothing but more hard rain, and I mean all night long. In the morning, getting out of the tent was a bitch because it was still raining and I had to stuff all of my gear back into the backpack. This is tricky when it so wet 'cause you have to make sure there is no seepage into the dry sacks. I experienced a trip in Alaska where it rained for twelve days straight. When it rains this much or even for a few days in a row, like on this trip, all of the gear will eventually get wet due to the rain sneaking in via your wet clothes, raincoat, and sweat. To make matters worse, in these types of conditions, condensation builds up in the tent during the night. If you happen to roll over and hit the side of the tent, the condensation falls like rain, getting everything wet. You try your hardest not to touch the sides, but in a small tent that is impossible when you are putting your pants and shirt back on. Fun stuff.

Once everything was packed, I headed for the cook tent to grab some food and stay dry before departure. It was still raining. Nothing warm to eat, only granola bars. Andy yelled out to the guys to convene a meeting. Our goal was to cross the river, get on the glacier, and make up for a lost day of travel. It was going to be a long day. I put my backpack on, and we started moving upstream. The waterfalls were flowing a little stronger and the river was higher than yesterday. The situation was actually *worse* than yesterday. How did we plan on crossing the river? It was deeper and the current was faster and stronger. I was getting concerned, but maybe Andy knew of a spot that was safe to cross. As we followed, Andy and I heard some strange sounds…rocks rolling down the river. Not small rocks, but rocks bigger than a basketball.

So how do we cross a river with a current strong enough to move big rocks, let alone when you cannot see the rocks coming at you under the water? The simple answer is *not* to cross the river. You wait. Patience in Alaska is vital to a hiker's success. Making matters worse, there were now chunks of ice flowing down the river. Chunks of ice that could easily break your leg if you got hit. I remember standing next to the river in amazement watching these chunks float by. *What the hell? Holy shit, that chunk was about three feet long.* Someone was going to lose a leg and/or get washed down the river.

I walked up around the corner to see how close we were to the glacier. It was only about 2,000 feet away. That explained the large ice chunks. What was even more impressive was the force of the water coming out from under the glacier. It was like seeing a tsunami being compressed into a confined area and then coming out from under the glacier with a tremendous amount of pressure. It was very intimidating to see and even worse considering the fact that we had to cross this roaring river. Another crazy concern came to mind. Could this amount of water flowing out of the glacier with such pressure cause caving? What is the potential of an internal glacier lake bursting into the river? My experience and gut feeling told me to hang back for another day. This did not happen.

As I was assessing the situation, I saw a wild man running up toward the glacier. It was Andy. *What in the heck was he doing?*

"Hey, what's up? Everyone drop your packs. I am going to find a place to cross this river."

He ran up to the glacier and could not find a good spot above us. Nor could Andy find a place for us to climb onto the glacier from the right side. It was too steep, and we did not have the proper climbing gear.

"Okay, guys, here in the plan of action. We are going to cross right here."

Really? I looked at the river and it was narrow in this particular spot, which was not good. The narrower the river, the stronger the current and the harder it will be to keep your feet planted on the bottom of the riverbed. I walked over to the edge of the river, looking and listening. I saw ice chunks and heard rocks rolling under the water. I was not sure this was a smart thing to do. I put my faith in Andy, thinking that he had experience in this part of Alaska. We prepared for the crossing, then put our backpacks on and started walking toward the river. As we were making our approach, I was talking with Kevin, a renowned Alaska photographer with a ton of Alaskan hiking experience, about the conditions of the river crossing. We both showed a great deal of concern but placed our faith in Andy. Kevin did mention that his biggest fear was death by freezing. Another concern was the fact that Andy did not go over the protocols of how to prepare for a river crossing and what do when crossing the river.

The standard protocol is to remove your boots and socks, put on river shoes, and lift up your pants above your knees. You get your boots, fill them with your socks, and tie them together and hang them around your backpack. This way, you have a boot hanging off your right and left sides. The most important aspect of prepping for river crossing is to unsnap your waist band and chest strap. The reason for doing this is to ensure that if you do go down in the river, the weight of the backpack does not push you down into the water and drown you. The next step is to get in a line, putting your hands on the backpack of the person in front of you. This creates a chain allowing each person to maintain the balance of the group. Finally, you enter the river at an angle to the river current.

None of these steps were addressed by Andy. What made matters worse was that Robert had never gone camping before, let alone crossed a raging river. As we approached the river, we lined up. It was Andy, then me, Robert, and finally Kevin. The first couple of steps into the water were extremely cold, to the point it felt like my feet were getting stabbed by a million needles. It hurt! We kept inching into the narrowest part of the raging river. The water was only halfway up to my knees and I could feel the power of the current. *This is going to be bad.* I heard some boulders bouncing down the river and was just waiting to get hit by one of them. Nothing yet!

Step after step the water was getting deeper and the current stronger. I was now up to the middle of my thighs and I was really leaning into the current. It was getting hard to maintain my footing. It seemed that every time I picked up a foot, I had to fight pretty hard to keep it from washing backward. What made it even harder were the rocks under my feet. They were uneven, round, and very unstable. This made it that much more challenging because I could not get a solid foot placement. I looked up to see how much farther we had to go to make it across. We still had three quarters of the way to go. The worst was yet to come. Oh shit! Step after step the water got deeper and the current got stronger. It now felt like I had a thousand pounds of pressure on my legs, *pushing, pushing, pushing.* Leg movement was now extremely difficult. Every time I picked up my leg to move forward it got washed backward and I felt the raging river trying to pick me up. At 6'3" and 230 pounds, you would think it would not be a problem to maintain contact with the riverbed. What about the other guys? They weighed no more than 175 pounds each. They must be floating already. The fight was on one hundred percent. This was now a fight for survival.

With a few more steps, the raging water was hitting Andy in the chest and hitting me just above my hips. I was literally pushing Andy forward against the current. A few more steps toward the middle of the river and Andy starts yelling.

"Push me down! Hold me in place!"

Andy was no longer in contact with the riverbed. He was floating. I held on and pushed down with all of my strength, but Andy was merely a bobber now. Within seconds, Andy's feet turned in the direction of the raging current, and I was actually holding Andy horizontally with his head pointing upstream. I held on as long as possible, but the current ripped him out of my hands. Andy was gone! The others were yelling but the sound of the raging river was so loud I could barely hear them.

"We need to get across!"

"No shit!" I yelled.

We never got a chance take another step. The river must have surged and the water rose to the level of my chest. My left foot was hit and ripped off the bottom of the river. I leaned into the surge. It felt like an elephant pushing on my chest. Then my right foot was taken out, and I went in headfirst with my hands out in front of me. Then Robert and Kevin lost their footing and fell into the river. All of us were now fighting for our lives.

When I fell into the river, the weight of the backpack pushed me hard to the bottom, hitting round and jagged rocks. I was on my hands and knees. After hitting the bottom, the current hit my chest and flipped me over backward before I started to roll down the river. After a couple of hundred feet of tumbling and rolling, I ended up on a small pile of rocks in the center of the river. I remember waking up on my back with the water lapping over my head. The world around me was now surreal with no sound or motion. I was in a mild state of shock due to the impact on the bottom of the river, tumbling, and the frigid cold water. *What just happened?* I had to tell myself over and over again that I had to get up. I had to get moving. It is time to survive. It felt like I was lying there forever.

When I started to gain full consciousness, I felt something tugging on my right arm. I looked to my right and my backpack strap was wrapped around my arm, stopping it from being taken by the river. Curling my arm, I pulled it out of the current, which gave me an opportunity to pull it onto the rocks on which I lay. I continued to say that I have to get up, I have to stand up.

Move, Patrick, move.

Placing my arms at my sides and into the water, I sat up and could not feel the water hitting my back. I rolled to the left, got to my knees, and finally stood up. Boy that hurt. The first thing I did was bitch about how bad everything hurt and how brutally cold I was. The water temperature was about thirty-five degrees. I did not hear any cries from Andy, Kevin, or Robert. I started scanning the banks of the river. I looked above me—nothing, then turned my attention downstream. I saw Andy on the left side sitting next to the river. He appeared to be okay. I found Robert a little farther down the river, standing, but confused and scared. I could not find Kevin. *Where did he go? Was he okay?* There he was on the other side of the river. He was injured and in pain, but I could not tell what was wrong. Everyone was alive.

With everyone still alive I had to focus on how I was going to get myself back to the left bank of the river. I picked up my backpack, threw one strap over my shoulder and looked at the river. *I have to cross this again?* I put the other strap over my shoulder and very carefully started to cross the river again. I was so cold that I could not feel my feet or the bone-chilling water at all. I knew this was bad news. Hypothermia was setting in. I took my first steps back into the raging river. The current caught my foot; I stumbled, caught my balance, and stopped. I was not going to fall in again. I proceeded; a rock hit my foot, and I almost fell in again. My nerves were getting the better of me, coupled with the fact that I could not feel my feet at all, but I made it. Once I got to the other side, I immediately stripped, dumped the contents of the backpack, and searched for the bright yellow dry sack that contained my emergency dry clothes. It was then that I noticed blood running down my left leg. I'd shredded my left shin down to the bone. What was really impressive were the size of the bumps on the bony part of my shin. They were the size of golf balls with blood coming out of the center of each one. I did not know the extent of the damage yet, so I put on my long johns. That was all I had for dry clothes. It was far from ideal, but it was good enough for the time being. When I was going through my gear, I noticed the river had taken my boots, gloves, trekking poles, water bottles, rain pants, and some other gear that was tied to my backpack. I was in tough shape, but not in the worst shape.

Kevin had almost drowned on this day. He forgot to unsnap his chest strap and could not free himself from his backpack. He was being pushed face down to the bottom of the river as he was being rolled and tumbled by the current. When he was finally able to get his head above water, he would take a breath before being pushed back down again. This happened a couple of times before the current of the river drove him to the shore. Once on the shore, you could see that he was choking and spitting up water. He was suffering, but alive. Andy, Robert, and I tried to find out the extent of our injuries. Andy, looking at my left leg, said it was broken.

"Can you walk on it? That cut goes right to your bone. What about your knee? It's swollen."

"I can move, so all is good for now. How are you guys?"

They all said they were doing okay. I could see that Robert was freezing and shivering hard.

Robert, the least experienced hiker in the group, made it through this disaster without any injuries but for the fact that he lost his entire backpack to the raging river. To lose your backpack is to lose your lifeline. He had no dry clothes to change into. We looked for it briefly, but we had to work on getting warm first. With Kevin in his tent across the river, the three of us found a big rock, sat down, and leaned against it trying to figure out what to do next. Robert and I never really sat down for long, as we kept walking back and forth to generate some heat. It helped but did not relieve the suffering. We were shivering hard, so hard that it hurt.

What struck me as a little strange was that Andy was not shivering. I was trying to figure out why. It all made sense now. Just after the crash into the river, I'd seen Andy putting water into his water bottle. I thought it strange, but he'd pulled out his cooking stove, boiled some water, put it into his bladder, and put the bladder under his coat. Andy did not offer the use of the hot, warm bladder to anyone, not even Robert. He needed it the most being that he had no gear at all, only the wet clothes on his back. A guide's first and foremost concern should be taking care of the hikers. This was not the case. Andy only cared about himself.

What I learned from this incident was that survival changes the nature of humans. When it comes down to who shall live or die, no one is your friend. Andy was initially out for only himself and did not care what happened to the others. This concerned me and changed my way of thinking. I needed to take some level of control of what happened next. We needed to get Kevin some form of communication device. So, being that we had superfluous communications systems, we wanted to give Kevin one. There was no way to get the satellite phone across the river. We could have thrown the phone, but the river was far too wide. We tried to communicate with Kevin via hand signals to confirm his overall condition. Kevin kept pointing at his ankle and indicated using his hands that his ankle was swollen. We could not see his ankle, but he was limping badly. Kevin hugged himself indicating that he was cold, waved, and headed into his tent.

Back next to the rock again, we were trying to figure out a game plan. Andy was obviously still shaken by the incident and was confused, but warm. Suddenly he looked up at me as if he saw a ghost and said, "Did you hit the emergency beacon on your inReach unit?" I said no. Andy was thankful. I am not sure why, but I think that he was embarrassed and was trying to figure out a way to explain it to the owner of the guide service. Misguided or what? His top concern should have been the fact that Robert was freezing cold, that Kevin was stranded on the other side of the river with an injured ankle, the fact that my legs were bleeding through my long johns, and both my shin and knee were swollen. This was not a big concern to him because Andy was warm.

After about an hour or so of leaning against the large rock, Andy called the owner of the guide service and told him, in part, what had happened. What I heard from the owner was him asking if we could complete the trip. Andy said, "We have two injured hikers. One hiker might have a fractured leg, a seriously swollen knee, and is bleeding. The other hiker is injured and stuck on the other side of the raging river. Robert and I are uninjured, but Robert lost all of his gear to the river."

"Well, Andy, can you get the injured hiker, Patrick, and Robert back to Turquois Lake before nightfall?"

"It is a six-hour hike, but we should be able to make it. What about Kevin?"

"There is not enough time to rescue Kevin tonight, but I will tell the bush pilot to bring a small inflatable raft and tomorrow morning you and another guide will have to hike back up to Kevin and get him across the river and back down to Turquoise Lake."

With a game plan set up, Andy, Robert, and I started our hike back down to the headwaters of Turquoise Lake. I was unable to bear additional weight on my left leg, so Robert who still had his boots, carried my backpack. I had no boots, trekking polls, or gloves as this gear was taken by the river. All I had for hiking were my open-toed river shoes with no socks. It was going to be a hard trip back. Before we got too far, we stopped at the river's edge across from Kevin's tent. We started yelling to Kevin. He popped out of the tent and we signaled to him that we were hiking out and will be back for him tomorrow. He did not like the idea, but we had no choice. The river was still raging and we needed a raft.

On the way back to Turquoise Lake, the sun finally came out, and boy did it feel good. The first time we came to a tributary stream, we attempted to avoid the cold water, being that I had no boots. The attempt failed and after that we just walked across the tributaries without consideration. It was very cold at first but after a couple of crossings my feet were so purple and numb that it did not matter anymore. We just had to get back to the headwaters and wait for the bush pilot and the raft. That was our sole focus.

At one point in the trip, we climbed a small hill that gave us a good view of the flowing river. I told Robert to keep an eye out for his backpack floating down the river. We did not think there was a chance, but a few minutes later, I heard, "Holy cow, there it is! I can see it." Sure enough, the backpack was moving fast and bobbing up and down like a bobber on a fishing pole. We all scrambled to the river's edge, chasing it down the river. At one point, it got hung up on a rock out of the main flow of the river. We tried to figure out a plan to get it, but the water was still running too fast. It broke free and we followed it down the river for the next hour or so. Once we reached the headwaters, the river widened greatly, giving us a chance to wade out and retrieve the backpack. We dragged it back across the river and set up a small camp along Turquoise Lake. Everything in the backpack was full of mud, stones, and water. Nothing was really salvageable.

It was now late in the afternoon, and the sun was starting to get low on the horizon. We did not have enough gear for all three of us, but we were making plans to share a tent, a sleeping bag, and what little food we had in the event we had to stay overnight. We did not anticipate getting picked up on this day. We waited for a while, and during this time Andy called the owner of the guide service to report our status. Andy was scared of the truth and did not want to disclose all of the details of what happened, such as making a bad decision to cross a raging river. The owner asked if anyone was good enough to finish a modified version of the trip. Andy indicated that my injuries were too bad to continue. Robert, on the other hand, was uninjured and able to continue. The only problem was that Robert had no viable gear. So, I gave him my gear so he could continue with his modified version of the trip. Just after we completed packing Robert's pack, we heard a plane coming up the lake. It was the rescue plane. I was super happy to the see the plane, because I knew that I would be flying back to Port Alsworth to start healing my wounds. Robert and Andy ended up staying for the night, and the next morning they hiked back up to Kevin. By the time they got back to Kevin, the water in the river receded and they were able to walk across the river to assist him. Later that day, while I was in Port Alsworth, Kevin showed up and was taken directly to Anchorage for medical attention. To this day, neither Kevin's ankle nor my knee have ever fully healed. You end up paying for your risk-taking at some point, and mine was during this trip. I think about Alaska every time I walk back to the barn.

During this entire fiasco, I'd completely forgotten about my Garmin inReach system, which has a tracking option. When using this option, you can allow your friends and family to track your progress via pre-set time intervals. For example, I had my tracking intervals set up to send tracking and mapping information every ten minutes. I know this is a short period, but if anything ever went wrong, it would be fairly easy to find me or my remains.

Anyway, several members of my family and my wife, Joanne, were tracking and watching this trip. For the first day, the tracking showed me going up the river valley. So, all was good. Then the tracks on the second day showed us going toward the river. After that, the tracking showed my movement in the areas of the crash going back and forth, and around in circles, and then no real movement. This is when I was leaning against the rock. At this point, there was no real concern as random movements are not a sign of a problem. So, no big deal for those that were tracking the trip.

Later in the evening after the river disaster, Joanne went to bed, but for some reason awakened and checked the inReach tracking information. Something was out of sorts. Why were my tracking points showing me hiking back toward Turquoise Lake? Joanne called my brother, Gary, and said something strange was going on. Gary said, "I know. Going back. That makes no sense." There was no immediate concern so they both went back to bed.

A couple of hours later, another call came in from Joanne to Gary. "So why is inReach showing Patrick moving at 130 mph?" Both became very concerned because now they both knew that something was definitely wrong. They were following the track of the plane for the next hour and fifteen minutes. It was heading back to Port Alsworth. They both knew something was wrong but did not know what had actually happened. Scary times. They tried calling my satellite phone, but that was turned off. They had no way of knowing what happened or if I was dead or alive.

They followed my tracker into Port Alsworth, followed me getting out of the plane, and saw my tracks heading toward a building. The building was my room for the night, thanks to the generosity of Glen Alsworth Jr. and his family. Once in the room, a nurse came over to check out my injuries to make sure they were not life threatening. If they were, there'd be an hour-and-a-half flight to Anchorage.

With my examination complete, it was determined that I had a serious injury to my meniscus, that I needed stitches, and a real stiff shot of whisky. So, I took some aspirin, turned off the Garmin inReach unit, and called Gary and Joanne to let them know that I had crashed in the river but that I was okay. I ended up staying in Port Alsworth for a couple more days to let my wounds heal before I ventured back into the real world. I truly appreciate Glen Alsworth taking the time to shuffle me around on his four wheeler, being that my knee was too painful to walk on. I almost died during this trip, but I was right back at it the following season and after my knee surgery. I am proud to say that I am reminded of this trip every day when I get that sharp pain running though my knee. This is an adventurer's trophy!

Story 3

The Charge

So, there I was at my office as the sun was coming up, poring over boxes of documents, letters, contracts, complaints, exhibits, regulations, laws, photos, interrogatories, depositions, and sooo much more. Why was I spending this grueling amount of time gathering and learning all of the factual and not-so-factual details of a legal case for which I was neither a plaintiff nor a defendant? That is a question I ask myself every day. So, like other days, I read, I took notes, created charts and flow diagrams, organized a logical progression of documents and alleged facts trying to justify an argument of persuasion based upon circumstantial evidence and legal bias attitudes. Fun stuff for sure!

You see, when you are an expert witness, you are brought into litigation late in the legal process. This means you have to get familiar with all the facts from the start of the original problem between the parties. Also, as the expert, you are fed only one side of the case, and you must assume what facts are relevant to the opposing side and how those facts will impact your opinion when writing the expert report and during cross examination. Generally, the expert witness is given the original complaint as a reliable document of facts upon which to opine. As we all know, a complaint is not a dissertation of facts, but only a slanderous iteration of falsehoods spattered with facts, which attorneys rely on as gospel. Getting through this mess of a legal system is no easy task, but it is essential to the financial viability of law firms.

So, with great advocacy for our legal system and to achieve justice for all, I endeavored to take on the not-so-easy task of writing an expert witness report to support the law firm's position—and my ass—so when I am crossed examined, the opposing legal counsel walks into a legal trap leading to settlement discussions.

This is not easy. Working week after week, day after day, hour after hour, I try to understand the legal foundation and how that can be expressed to the judge and jury. My client in this case was a substantial law firm that had a reputation for winning at any cost. This makes the work even harder and more detailed and takes a great deal of time and dedication. Time and effort which translates into billable time for me, which is marked up three-fold by the law firm. Don't forget that success in a law firm is dictated by the amount of billable time. The more time you bill, the more likely you are to become a partner. Money translates into success, not the wellbeing of the client.

Well, anyway, there I was, thinking about how much client information I had to read, then thinking about Alaska, thinking about the arguments I had to develop and defend, then thinking about Alaska, shifting back to the expert report, saying I had to focus—otherwise I will get my butt kicked during my deposition…But I started thinking about Alaska again. Okay, the hell with it!!! I turned to my other computer and typed in "Alaska Alpine Adventures" and started sifting through their website. The back-country guide service takes you places such as Lake Clark National Park, Gates of the Arctic National Park, and many other remote places in Alaska. It is a very cool and intriguing site.

So, for the next couple of weeks, as I was developing the expert report, I frequented the Alaska Alpine Adventures website and was drawn to Alaska's challenges and beauty. My desire to book a trip was strong, but I held back, as my responsibilities with running a successful government contract consulting firm were what held me back. Maybe in my next life I will go on one of these amazing trips.

With the thoughts of Alaska behind me, I worked ten-hour days for a couple of weeks, and the last seventy-two hours without a break in order to complete the expert report on time for the law firm to review and submit. It was a good report with a new, irrefutable argument, which the law firm missed, due to discrimination and failure to award to a Mexican-owned small business. Law firms never give you enough time to review all of the pertinent documents. This is done in order to manage the expert witness arguments—not a very reasonable process at all.

Upon submission of the report to the law firm, I received a call from the chief legal counsel. She wanted to talk about the report. During this discussion, we went over the basic arguments, which were defendable. Then when we got to the discrimination portion of the expert report. Counsel started making suggestions about making changes to the argument, ultimately directing me to change my expert report by deleting the discrimination arguments. WHAT?!!!

"So, counsel, I ask, you want me to destroy my original report, redraft it, and then submit a second *signed* report for submission to the court?"

Counsel replied, "Yep!"

In the world of expert report writing, you as the expert are put under oath to attest to the fact that you had no outside help, support, influence, or suggestions incorporated into the report from undisclosed contributors.

I then asked, "How, when I am put under oath, am I to address the fact that counsel wanted to alter my expert witness testimony?"

Counsel said, "There is no reason to let the opposition know that I made this suggestion."

WHAT!!!?

I told Counsel that I would have to think about her suggestion and get back with her in a few. My first thought was to go to the Alaska Alpine Adventure website to get away from our discussion and think with a clear mind. As I was looking through all the adventures, I paid attention to the vast wilderness and what it offers. Here is what came to mind: The wilderness is a vast, beautiful place with endless challenges, endless fun, and endless heartache. What connects the challenges, fun, and heartache is the unwavering truth that is offered by the vast wilderness. A truth that lets you know when you make mistakes, and when you do something right or wrong. A truth with no excuse or hidden agenda. You live or die by your decisions. In other words, the wilderness is the most honest place in the world. There's no convoluted bullshit as there is with legal battles. With the inspiration of looking at this Alaska Alpine Adventure website, I found a place that I wanted to visit for twelve days on a solo backpacking trip that would take me into the middle of nowhere. A place that is only reachable by float planc. I made a few calls that afternoon and booked my trip with a backcountry bush pilot. The trip was on for early September.

After some additional planning, I clearly remember walking onto a small plane in my hometown knowing that my adventure would bring endless challenges and fun—and endless heartache. As the plane started taxiing down the runway, it was like the start of being transported into a different dimension. A dimension that kept on getting more intense as I traveled to Detroit, Minnesota, and then landed in Anchorage.

After landing in Anchorage, I checked into the Merrill Field Inn. I got a good night's rest and the next morning headed to a small airport; the bush flight capital of the world. I then boarded a six-seater plane that took me to Port Alsworth, the small bush town in Lake Clark National Park, where I'd set out from on my encounter with the roaring river. There is no other way to access Port Alsworth but for a bush plane. After spending the night in Port Alsworth at the Lake Clark Lodge, I boarded a four-seater bush plane equipped with floats. The seriousness of the trip was now upon me as I watched the tundra below streak by. I would soon be at the drop-off point that I could only imagine a few months ago. A place imagined based upon the truth that it offered, and the honesty that told me to submit the original report.

I was now past the point of no return as I entered the final leg of my dimensional change from the world of the less-spoken truth to the world of absolute truth. I stepped out of the float plane onto the shore of a distant lake that offered nothing of our social world. All that was around me were challenges, fun, heartache, and the absolute truth. It is very hard to face the truth one hundred percent of the time.

On this first night, I was surrounded by cliffs to my right and left, a huge river valley in front of me, and a lake behind me. I heard nothing but unresponsive echoes as I set up my camp and laid out my gear. The truth of the matter was I had no control of what would happen next. With the truth yet to be exposed, I grabbed my cooking stove and made some dehydrated Mountain House food—you know—just add water. Yuck! And some warm hot chocolate. A great meal indeed. My plan for the next day was unknown, but that felt good. I jumped in my sleeping bag, closed my eyes—not really—and fell asleep thinking of poppy seeds, Christmas trees, and Santa Claus. Now THAT is NOT the truth!!! I did keep the toilet tissue nearby, just in case I was scared shitless during the night.

With a bit of frost in my sleeping bag, I woke the next morning freezing my ass off, but the magnificence of all that was around me humbled my discomfort of the situation, and I made some powdered eggs and some more hot chocolate. On a typical morning I would shit, shower, and shave, but there was no reason to shower or shave, and I could not really shit due to the lack of food. So, with unfettered inspiration I grabbed my day pack and headed up the valley surrounded by huge cliffs. As I was walking up this river valley, which was maybe a mile or so wide, I was paying attention to all the tributaries that led off to other dimensions. One looked like it reached to the heavens, and others looked foreboding and desolate. After about four hours of hiking up this valley, I was getting comfortable with my surroundings and started to relax. There was a 650-foot spire that was in the center of the riverbed and with my confidence intact, I decided to climb to the top. This was a bigger challenge than I thought, but I made it. I was becoming a confident explorer. While I was sitting on the top looking down at the riverbed, I noticed a white flash to my right. I could not find out what it was, but I kept on looking and sure enough, a group of mountain goats were cautiously watching me.

With my sweat starting to cool off, I decided it was time to get off the spire and back to the river valley. I could not go the way I'd come as it was too steep to climb down. Did I make a mistake?!!! Confidence gone!!! I looked around and decided to head down the steepest side of the spire, as it offered better foot and hand placements. It was a nerve-racking descent. One mistake and I would have plunged into the freezing cold waters of the river below. It came close a few times, but with God at my side, I made it down. This was fun, but I'd almost made a deadly mistake. There is no room for mistakes when you are alone in the Alaskan outback. There is also no room for cockiness.

After getting back to camp, just before sunset, I ignited my cook stove, boiled some water, poured in dehydrated beef and vegetables, waited a few minutes, and dinner was served. Another great meal from Mountain House foods. For dessert was a Hershey bar. Now *that* was good. With a full belly, I sat and watched the remnants of the day's light holding onto the landscape, changing colors from red to orange to amber to blue, and green. It was a great battle of light versus darkness, and the showdown was absolutely amazing. But darkness arose from the forest, and once again brought the realm of night back to this place on Earth. With night upon me, I crawled into my sleeping bag, fluffed up my backpack in lieu of a pillow, gently closed my eyes, and opened my ears to listen to the night's songs composed of unacknowledged sounds.

These songs are truly mesmerizing and really tickle the soul. Let me warn you: if during one of these mesmerizing songs you hear a crack, growl, thundering steps, or a howl, I suggest that you say your prayers, grab your bear spray or your gun, get the hell out of the tent if you have time, and start yelling "HEY BEAR" or something to scare off the animal that is ready to quash their appetite. On this night, I was blessed with the mesmerizing music of the night and was not the focus of any animal's appetite.

With the night behind me, I gathered all my gear and planned on heading toward the lake. I had a choice to make, as one side of the lake was steep and full of alders as far as I could see. The other side of the lake had experienced a landslide at some point in the past and was only covered with rocks and scree. So, with the choice made, I headed toward the left side of the lake to challenge the rocks.

It was pretty easy going for the first two hours, as most of the rocks were firmly in place and posed no real danger of shifting underfoot, of feet getting trapped, or starting an avalanche. There were though, ample places to fall, likely without taking your head off or breaking any bones. But all of this rapidly changed. For the next couple of hours, the rock-fall area became very unstable and was constantly shifting under my feet. I was worried about starting an avalanche. If you lost your balance in this area, you would fall directly into protruding rocks with crevasses deeper than the length of my arms. This meant if you fell, you would be stopped by the sharp edges of the rocks, or fall into a hole between boulders that would not allow you to push yourself out. If I fell to my right, I would hit boulders, roll into the lake, and then sink into the water at a depth of 800 feet. I've heard that seventy-pound backpacks are not very buoyant.

I was in grave danger; to make a mistake would be deadly. To manage the perils of the rocks, I had to plan my movement with great detail. Flirtatious movements could result in me hitting my emergency radio beacon— if conscious—for help. This is something I did not want at all. So, imagine if you will, walking on a swinging slack line for a mile or more without falling off. This is what it was like for hours. I would literally have to jump from rock point to rock point, meaning there was not enough room at any point during this traverse to place my feet fully on any one stone. What made it worse was the fact that each stone was not stable and would move under my feet. I only had moments to get off a rock before it would roll away from under my feet. It was a dangerous time indeed. I was extremely happy to get off the rocks and onto solid land again. I was never so focused in my life.

Once out of the rocks, I took off my pack, grabbed some water from my water bottle, and chewed on a candy bar while looking back at the rock field, then looking at the alders across the lake. *Had I made the right decision?* Well, I guess that I did, because I did not get hurt. Deep down, I knew that I'd taken an unreasonable chance. I have learned once again that taking a chance in the wilderness can be deadly. This is the second time that I had taken an unreasonable risk and was lucky enough to survive. Would the next risk be my third strike? I did not know, and did not want to find out. I would be more cautious from then on.

The next couple of hours of hiking were easy, but I kept on thinking of the rock field. I replayed in my mind how many times my feet had rolled off the rocks, the times that I stumbled, and the fear of falling into the 800-foot deep lake. Boy, if I'd fallen into the lake, they would never have found me. Or even worse, never know what had happened to me. They would say that I disappeared in the formidable Alaskan Triangle, which has consumed over 16,000 souls. I would become a legend!!! NOPE, that is no fun at all. I would rather be a lone hiker with stories to tell in my elder years than a water-logged legend. Righty OOOOH!!!

I finally reached the end of the lake and decided to set up camp on the far reaches of a little spit extending about 300 feet into the lake. This way I was partially protected on three sides by water and only had to worry about a bear coming into camp from one direction. Feeling safe, I set up camp, pulled out my camping chair, and relaxed for the first time all day. It was a tough day for sure, but it was fun, exciting, and painfully challenging. Still hungry after my Mountain House scrambled eggs (yuck) I walked off the "spit" and started looking for my favorite Alaskan food, wild blueberries. I looked and looked, but it was too early in the season. Just as I was returning from my blueberry search, I noticed some old bear tracks about halfway down the spit. The prints were very, very big, meaning it was a grizzly. I would assume that a grizzly was looking for salmon or a good fish dinner. I just had to make sure the grizzly would not enjoy a good Polish kielbasa dinner if he returned tonight. Thus, my moments of relaxation were now gone, and survival was back on. I got back to camp, gathered all my food and stinky stuff into the food barrel, closed it, and then stored it away from camp. The hope is the bear will eat the food barrel and not the kielbasa. Time would tell.

With the morning sun beating on my tent and a nice cold chill blowing down the lake, I decided to venture outside the tent to heat up some water for hot chocolate and oatmeal. The hot chocolate was great! As I was sipping the hot chocolate, I had no specific route for the day. I said to myself, *I will let the mountains decide*, and sure enough, they did. The mountains highlighted a pass through the mountain range that headed to my eventual pick-up point at Twin Lakes. The ascent to the pass was going to take some work, but it could not be any harder than the rock field.

During my ascent to the pass, I would often wonder what would be on the other side. A cliff that goes down to the valley below, a lake, more mountains to climb, a glacier, a giant grizzly bear? I had no idea at all, but the excitement that compelled me up the mountain was felt in every step and placement of my trekking poles. Never once did I get tired; rather, as the anticipation grew, the frequency of my steps quickened. It was absolutely thrilling. As I entered the pass, I was guided by very large mountains to the north and south that had been non-existent during my ascent. It was almost as if these mountains were part of a mystical fantasy where their existence was visible only when they were being looked at directly. It was truly strange, and yes, mystical. Before I got swallowed by the pass, I stopped, turned around, and looked at the lake from which I came and the surrounding area.

It was like looking at a different world or dimension. Things were about to change. I could feel it in my heart and soul. I turned back toward the pass with enthusiasm as clouds moved in and filled the pass. I could not see very far in front of me, so I walked with caution. And then—a sound.

I paused for a few minutes to try and determine what I was hearing. It sounded like a roar or rustling, and then a few seconds later I was hit by a fairly strong gust of wind. A wind that must have come from the valley that was concealed by the clouds in which I was engulfed. The wind as it lapped around my body felt like the spirits of the gods and all those that have gone before me. It was very uplifting and offered me an absolute sense of freedom without fear. I now knew that I was protected, loved, and blessed. I'd never really had this feeling before, even though I have been trying to find it for decades. I think the key was being alone with myself and Mother Nature, where there is nothing but the absolute truth. Like a great person once said:

"Where there is fear there is no truth and where there is no truth there is no you."

Written by Patrick Malyszek

With all of this cool stuff going on, it felt like I had a new connection to the earth and the spirits of the earth. So, with a new-found sense of freedom, I stretched my foot out and took a step into my new world. With this step and the steps to follow, I noticed the clouds were starting to clear and what was presented before me was utterly amazing. I saw an endless expanse of large stones, rolling hills, large mountains speckled with white, and a river flowing far in the distance. Had I not entered the pass I never would have seen this new world and all its magnificence. OH MY GOD!!!

Exhausted from the physical and mental exertions, I found a big boulder, climbed it, took a seat on top, and broke out a Hershey bar and some water. There was not a chance in hell that I was going to spoil these moments with Mountain House food. No way!!! So, after the Hershey bar was gone, I lay back on the boulder and basked in the sun for a couple of hours. Boy, that felt good!!! All rested, I packed things up and started following my feet again. I only had a couple of hours left before the battle of the skies started again (light v. darkness), so I decided to follow a small river stream that would take me higher into the mountains and position me to get into the Twin Lakes basin. This meant another pass, and I could not wait. *Maybe this one will take me to Mars.* You never know. Seriously, you never really know.

Walking up this small river stream was not really that hard, as the vegetation was only about knee height and there were no seven-foot alders to work through. With the ease of the day a blessing, I noticed that I was getting to the origins of the small river stream as I walked into a mountain horseshoe. Once I got to this point, I realized it was time to find a place to set up camp for the night, put up the cook tent, and get ready for dinner. Before starting the stove, I set up my camp chair facing the towering mountains and gazed upon the kaleidoscope of colors. In one spot, not too far from camp, I noticed a dark black color that did not really fit in with the environment. After a short study, I determined I was looking at a hole in the side of the mountain. The next question was who made the hole and why? With a dangerous sense of curiosity, I grabbed my bear spear, which is supposed to work better than a gun, crossed the river, and started up the slope just below the hole. As I got closer, I noticed that some dirt surrounding the hole was relatively fresh. Was it a bear den? Did I scare the bear away and was I now being watched by the bear? I had no idea, but my dangerous sense of curiosity only grew. I walked directly in front of the hole, got down on my knees with great anticipation, and did not see a bear…so I decided to crawl into the four-foot diameter hole. I was about three feet in before the tunnel narrowed to the point that I could not go any deeper. There was not much to see, but I did find remnants of what I believe were a ground squirrel. My guess is that a determined bear was hungry enough to pursue a squirrel, at all costs, in order to resolve its hunger pains. I am sure glad I was not the subject of the bear's hunger pains. Even though I should have not ventured up to the hole I was happy that I had, as I would be able to sleep better knowing the hole was not an active bear's den.

I got back to camp, plopped into my chair, broke out the camp stove, heated up some water, and made some macaroni and cheese with reindeer sausage and hot chocolate. It was an amazing meal for sure. Before the light of day vanished, I gazed upon the mountains and saw about ten or fifteen white spots. These white spots turned out to be mountain goats. What is amazing is how white they are and how much they stand out. They are amazing creatures. So far, my interaction with wildlife had been a few bear tracks and some mountain goats. Oh, I cannot forget the dead squirrel. So far, so good!

It was time to hit the sleeping bag and call it a night.

So, I got up from my camp chair with grunts and groans, did a final scan of the wilderness, looking for any unsuspecting visitors, didn't see anything, unzipped the tent, then the sleeping bag, got in, and zipped everything up again. Then I could relax. It took me about an hour or so to get warm again, but when I stopped shivering, it was lights out. Well, just as I was warming up and getting comfortable, I heard a sound. Oh shit!!!

I listened intently trying to figure out what I'd just heard. I didn't have a clue as to what it might be. My first thought was a bear. I waited for about fifteen minutes or so and I heard no further sounds. Just when I thought the threat was over, I heard a grunt right next to my tent. OH MY GOD!!! It was not just right next to my tent—it was actually *pushing* on my tent. I was going through the sniff test. The animal was trying to figure out if I was going to be the appetizer, main course, or dessert. Holy shit!!! Seconds seemed like days, and minutes felt like years. What was going to happen?!!! What made matters worse was the fact that my hands were tucked into the sleeping bag and the zipper was all the way up to my nose. I was stuck in my mummy of a sleeping bag. I could not move. I was defenseless. If I passed the sniff test, I could be the first Polish meal this animal ever had. Pigs in the blanket, which is meat wrapped in cabbage. Yuck!!! *Oh My God.* I started feeling bad for this animal, because pigs in the blanket is horrible food. What, really? Yep, this time I'd lost it for sure. What a stupid but funny thought. I forced myself not to laugh.

Still stuck in my mummy of a sleeping bag, I was thinking of what my first move would be. *Do I unzip my sleeping bag? Do I fish my arms out of the sleeping bag? What do I do when my arms are free? Do I reach for the zipper on the tent? Do I grab the bear spray first?* So many moves, all of which take time and make a lot of noise. *Will all my movement and noise in the tent provoke an attack, or will the animal be scared away? What was going to happen? Wait! I forgot about the toilet paper. When do I grab that? It might be needed here shortly. Hold on, hold on*, I tell myself. Everything was going to hell in a handbasket.

After a great deal of constructive contemplation and laying out a plan of action of how I was going to save myself, I finally picked the solution. The solution that would save my life. This is exactly what I did: I stayed in the sleeping bag and did not move an inch. Was this a strategy? I would like to think so, but I really had no other option at that point. So, stuck in sleeping bag, I laid there watching the walls of the tent and listening for any more sounds or movement. It was totally silent. I waited another hour, and it was still quiet. Another hour or so went by and all was silent in the night. I think I made it. I did the right thing. The animal would not get its first taste of pigs in the blanket. No Polack for you, you bastard.

The morning silence was broken by the zipper of the sleeping bag being pulled down, then some ruffling, scratching, and pulling my feet out. The mummy had awakened with numb arms and legs from not moving most of the night. With great expectation, I reached for the bear spray with one hand and grabbed the zipper of the tent with the other. I started to pull up the zipper. What would I see? The anticipation was palpable. With my head sticking out of the tent, I looked to my right, then my left. I saw nothing. I got to my hands and knees, crawled out and away from the tent, and then stood up to get a better view of the surroundings. It was all clear—thank God! I looked around the tent trying to find evidence of the animal that was doing the sniff test. Sure enough, I saw tracks. It was not a bear at all! It was a moose walking around the tent trying to figure out what had popped up in its territory.

I was fortunate that it was a moose and not a bear. A bear would have gone after the pigs in the blanket, but a moose, on the other hand, is not that aggressive unless it is scared or threatened. I was told that moose cause more deaths than bears by stepping on and spearing those that threaten them. I can believe that, as I own a horse farm and horses can easily trample you to death if you are not careful. So, ultimately the fact that I did stay in my tent and did not move was really the right thing to do. Who knows?

So far on this trip I had seen bear tracks, mountain goats, was scared by a moose, and of course saw a dead squirrel. What was next, a bear? I hoped not! With the excitement behind me for now, I had Mountain House scrambled eggs and of course, hot chocolate. The breakfast of kings. My route this day would take me up a very steep fifty-six degree embankment for the first 600 feet of elevation gain. It was going to be hard work for sure. This route did not really have a mountain pass; rather, it was a plateau that would gradually ascend mile after mile. It was not a bad hike at all, but it was very grueling and long. After reaching the top of the mountain, I was able to see Twin Lakes in the distance. I anticipated it would only take a couple of hours at best to get to the edge of the lake. This was not the case at all. The descent into Twin Lakes turned from little to no vegetation to knee high alders, and for the final couple of miles, full grown brush, alders, and pine trees. It was a lot of work, but fun. What amazed me when I was hiking the final mile or so to the edge of the lake was how many deep holes and creeks I found. The creeks were mostly covered by vegetation and the water was probably five feet deep. I can see now why so many people go missing in Alaska. If you fall into one of these creeks or holes, no one would be able to find you.

I finally got to the edge of the lake and found a nice soft spot and set up camp. The spot I found was covered in moss and soft tundra grass. It was the best place ever.

After a quick meal, I headed into my tent to get away from the cold wind coming off the lake and to rid myself of the chill I had after cooling off from my hike. This sequence of events is fairly important because you use the heat you generate from hiking to ensure your warmth when setting up your tent and preparing your food. This way, you can generally avoid developing a chill which could lead to hypothermia. So, with all the chores done, I jumped into my sleeping bag to merely relax and enjoy the lack of physical activity. It was not long before I passed out. I awoke a few hours later, got up for a moment to take a leak, and got right back into the sleeping bag before all of the warmth went away. It was a gentle night with no real concerns of strange noises or animals trying to get into my tent. I was actually in the tent for a solid ten hours. It was so stinking comfortable. It was actually the best night of sleep I ever had in my life. The ground was so soft it felt like I was being hugged ever so gently. Amazing!!!

The only reason I got up the next morning was because I had to go to the bathroom. If it was not for that, I would have stayed in the tent even longer. Also, the bush pilot was supposed to pick me up sometime this morning, so I had to be ready. After filling my belly with Mountain House food and hot chocolate, I started to get my things together. I knelt down in front of the opening of my tent, leaned in, and started to organize my gear. After a few minutes, my sixth sense kicked in like a tsunami hitting a beach. I tried to ignore what I was feeling, but then the hair on the back of my neck stood up. I knew that something was up. I pulled back out of the tent, looked over the top, and sure enough, my sixth sense was spot on. About forty-five feet from my tent was a large grizzly bear with its head down, foraging in a blueberry patch. Time froze as everything around me started to move in slow motion. The alders seemed to flicker, the trees stood motionless despite the wind, and I could no longer feel the cold breeze coming off the lake. While still on my knees, I turned toward the lake, trying to find the easiest means of getting there. I figured that if I made it to the lake, I would have options. The first was to jump into the cold water of Twin Lakes. Not a very good idea as I stood a chance of freezing to death. The second option was to use the five-foot wide cobblestone beach, which is free from brush, as a means of trying to run away from the grizzly. As we all know, it is pretty much impossible to out a run a grizzly, but at least it was an option.

As I turned back toward the grizzly, I could see that I'd caught its attention. I stood up facing the grizzly, and I could see the wind rippling through its blonde, faded sun-bleached fur. At least I hoped it was the wind and not a charge in the making. I took a few steps back, turned, and headed for the cobblestone beach. As I was walking, I took several looks over my shoulder. The bear was not moving. Maybe I was safe. Well, I was not that lucky.

The grizzly started walking in my direction. Once I got to the lake, I stopped, paused, and then started walking up the beach away from the last location of the intruder. There was no visible sign of the grizzly. I continued for about twenty-five feet, stopped, turned, and checked once again. This time the grizzly was on the beach. It first looked away from me down the beach. I was thankful—but wait—the bear started to slowly turn. We were now looking at each other again. I am sure the bear was wondering whether or not I would be the morning meal. I hoped not, but if I was, all of my stored carbs should give it a heart attack. OOOOH justice is sweet. In this case, not really; for the bear to die of a heart attack would mean that I would become bear steak. Not a good idea at all.

As we stood facing each other, I was slowly taking steps backward. The more steps I took, the more time I had to devise a plan of action. Okay, so what is my plan? I grabbed my handgun out of the holster to look it over and ensure it was still loaded. Sure enough, it looked ready. I noticed movement, and the grizzly was now walking toward me. I held my ground as the grizzly continued to walk toward me. Was this going to be the end? With less than seventy-five feet between us, I noticed the front legs flare out and the hair stand up on the bear's back. The charge had started.

The bear was coming toward me as fast as it could. My heart was racing; my feet were telling me to run, but I knew to run would be sure death. I raised the gun and pointed it toward the charging bear. I pulled the trigger and there was a big BOOOOOOM. The bear was still coming at full force. I pointed the gun to the right of the bear, pulled the trigger. BOOOOOOOOOM.

You see, the first shot in the handgun was a blank, the purpose of which is to scare off a bear without causing injury. The second shot was nothing but buckshot. I did not want to hit the bear with buckshot, as that would only piss off the bear and guarantee an attack. So far, no luck. I had my finger on the trigger for the third shot, containing a slug. But it was too late. I did not have time to pull the trigger. The bear was at my side, only about two feet away, and I braced for impact. My life did not flash before my eyes, as some people say. All I saw were the eyes of the bear looking at me. The impact never happened. Holy poop!!! The bear just ran by me. Was the bear going to attack me from behind? I spun like a top, and to my amazement the bear was now merely walking in the other direction. The bear paused, turned its head in my direction, stopped for a few seconds, then continued on its way. I swore as God is my witness the bear said, *Today is your lucky day.* I was absolutely blessed on that day. The bear could have torn me apart. Life is truly amazing, as every moment is an adventure, and we never know how the adventure will turn out.

With the excitement thought to be over for the day, I sat down on a large stone and watched the bear walk away into the distance. When the bear faded into the rolling hills, I headed back to my tent, packed up my gear, and waited for the bush pilot. As I was waiting on the shores of Twin Lakes, watching the skies and listening for a plane, I heard something other than a plane. I listened intently. Oh!!!

I placed my head into my hands. Now what was going to happen? The sound I heard was a pack of wolves coming up the valley toward my location. There was no way that I could defend myself from a pack of wolves. I was in trouble for sure. I picked up my pack and started heading down the lake. I figured it would be better to start moving in lieu of staying in one place. I had to make sure I did not travel too far, otherwise the bush pilot would never find me. Only fifteen minutes into my walk, I heard the float plane coming up the valley. As it was taxiing to the shoreline, my anticipation grew and I was watching the woods, waiting for something to jump out and grab me. With haste I threw my backpack into the float plane, jumped in myself, and closed the door. I was finally safe and could not wait to get back to Port Alsworth.

In terms of my expert witness report, I re-emailed my original report, unchanged, back to the law firm. It was not received well, but the report was submitted to the court. Needless to say, the law firm was dismissed from the case and new counsel was retained by the Mexican-owned small business.

Story 4

The Unknown

As I walk into the wilderness of my backyard, located in Upstate New York, I am inspired by the beauty of the night sky and all the stars that are being offered to assist with my imagination and the expectations of my dreams. To stay immersed within this moment, I gather branches, sticks, and large pieces of wood. I am going to have a fire. In preparation, I take the small twigs and break them up with cracks, pops, snaps, and sometimes an ouch or two. The snapping of the twigs on this night becomes rhythmic and enchanting as the sounds they make are taking me away from reality and bringing me to a place where my heart is unencumbered within a world full of purities beyond my words of description.

After a momentary pause for introspection, I continue my efforts to build what is soon to be a fire into a fine-looking stack of wood. I finally get to the point where I am ready to start the fire. I strike a match, and its glow highlights a small portion of the world around me, reflecting in my eyes with an exhilarating sense of adventure. With the small flicker of a flame within the hollows of the stack of wood, I sit back and gradually watch the fire grow and fend off the darkness that once surrounded the place upon which I sit. As this great battle of light versus darkness ensues, I see the flames make shapes, some of which I have seen in the past on my great adventures. Then one great flame flares and I am instantly hurtling toward the stars above. Without knowledge of my destination, I am not fearful; rather, I am full of expectation and joy. I close my eyes for just a moment, which feels like a lifetime, and then without expectation and a little bump and bounce, I land. I open my right eye very slowly. First, I see a large, dark shape. Thinking it is a bear, I scream, but it is only a large boulder. I gradually open my other eye, and I see tall, green pine trees. Farther in the distance, I see a lake and very large mountains covered with snow... OOOOOOOH my gosh, can it be true? I AM IN ALASKA?! On one of my great adventures. I can smell the trees, pines, and fresh water running in the river…but which one of my adventures am I on?

***

With a wet mist hitting my face, I ponder with great strain, but at this moment I cannot figure it out. With surprise I hear a roar; it's an engine of a float plane moving away from the shore and throttling up to take off. As I look at the plane, I can feel the mist hitting my face.

Then, as the float plane gradually drifts into the distant clouds, my soul settles into the realm of silence and solitude, but this time something is different, something is wrong, but what?!!! No need to worry, as time will figure it out.

With the float plane gone, I grab my map to review my route that will take me through unknown valleys, over great mountains, forging through white water rivers, and weave me through mountain goats, giant brown and black bears, wolves, moose, and other majestic creatures. After confirming my route, which is merely an "I hope so," a "well maybe," an "I'll figure it out when I get there," or a "just head in that direction," (Yep, you guessed it, the map is worthless for showing what is in store for me on this trip) after all of this figuring is done, I securely stow the map into my backpack with a tug and a zip, never to be seen again. Then, with a grab of my hand, the backpack becomes weightless, and it flies into the air over my shoulders then onto my back as I stumble backward toward the lake. It was close, but there is no splash. UGGGGH, weightless, my ass! It weighs over seventy pounds. Yep, I do believe in lightweight hiking!

With the load of the backpack securely in place, I take my first steps in "that direction," which is climbing the majestic mountain that surrounds the lake. I look up and say to myself, *I can be at the top before nightfall*. As I start walking with great happiness and pride, I hear an unrecognizable noise that fails to amuse but has me a little concerned. I continue with my trek, and I hear, "This is too heavy. Can you carry some of the weight?" The silence and solitude are shattered. I turn around and I see what made the unrecognizable sound, and sure enough, it's Bob. WHAT! I AM THAT TRIP...? OOOOOOOH FUDGE!!!

Who is Bob, you ask? Do you really want to know?!!! Well, Bob has been a friend of mine since high school and we have had some good times over the years. On this particular Alaskan journey, my family did not want me to do a solo trip in the outback of Alaska as I have done previously. So, begrudgingly, I asked Bob if he wanted to go on the trip. Originally, he said no, but after a while he agreed to go. OUCH!!!

So, the plan of action was to fly up separately to Anchorage and meet at the Merrill Field Inn. I arrived at the Merrill Field Inn a day early so I could get prepared for the trip in terms of food, buying some last-minute items, and getting mentally prepared. Bob was scheduled to arrive sometime the following day. So, during this time of silence and solitude, which is something I cherish beyond understanding, I simply started thinking about the rhythm of my heart, walking through the brush, rain, snow, and the sound of the wind blowing across the great Alaskan plains into my face. Absolute heaven!!! I so looked forward to the approaching adventure that I could not stop smiling.

Then, like a giant clash of thunder, there was a knock, then a bang, and a "HELLOOOO, you in there?" The silence and solitude were gone but, hey, it was Bob, and I was glad to see him and knew that he made it safely to Anchorage. Before I had a chance to get out one sentence, Bob decreed that I had to leave the hotel room NOW because he just picked up a stewardess that was on his flight and he wanted to use the room for a couple of hours.

"WHAT? Are you kidding?" I asked Bob.

"Yes, she is a real nice girl with blonde hair and an amazing body. Pat, just leave for a while and I will give you more details later."

I paused, looked around, and said, "I don't see any amazing stewardess."

"PAT, she is coming here for sure so please just leave."

"You dumbass, you just got played by the stewardess. She will never show. If she actually shows up, I will relocate myself for a couple of hours. Promise!"

So, Bob, with an overload of testosterone, talked about how she served him while on the plane by bringing food, water, headphones, and a pillow. WHAT?!!! Serving passengers is part of her job. An hour went by and during this time Bob was chanting how beautiful she was and that she would be showing up shortly. Another hour went by, and I was laughing so hard that I could not catch my breath, but Bob was still confident that his soon-to-be lover—well maybe not his lover—would show up. Another hour went by, and this time Bob was checking his cell phone, walking around the parking lot of the hotel, watching every taxi, in hopes that she would appear. During the last hour of Bob's misguided expectations, he realized that he might have to resort to an alternate means of satisfaction. NO. NOT THAT… and…YES…IT GOT WORSE!!!

As I watched Bob walking around in the parking lot, I noticed that his shoulders were now drooping, and his head was down as he started walking back to the hotel room. He'd finally given up on his stewardess. I was laughing hysterically, but wait…a taxi pulled into the hotel parking lot and Bob with a jump of excitement started walking toward it with such haste it looked like he was ready to attack. The taxi stopped, the door opened ever so slowly and, sure enough, a lady started getting out. The taxi door obstructed the view, but first you saw her leg stretching out, then her arm, and then she clutched the taxi door and gradually rose to an erect position. Bob was excited. Her long, faded dress dropped off her knees, so gently hiding Bob's long-awaited prize. Her hair caught a little bit of wind and fluttered. I saw Bob tense up with his hands stretched out. What in the hell was he trying to do? I assumed his testosterone-clouded mind told him her fluttering hair was a butterfly in distress, and he wanted to be heroic and give this beautiful creature a place to land. His stewardess needed to be saved by her prince.

The pain was immense, unbearable, it was nothing like I have ever felt before, and I was getting worried. How to do I stop this massive discomfort in my stomach, back, throat, my whole body? It hurt. What do I do? Then another round of pain hit like lightning hitting a tree. All that I saw was an old lady in her eighties with thinning white hair standing next to the taxi door looking at Bob with baffled eyes. I swore to God that she thought she was going to get lucky. I yelled to Bob, "Is that the stewardess? Should I leave now and come back in a couple of hours?!" I was just about puking at this point from laughing so hard. Then, in no uncertain terms and with some foul language I heard, "That is not the one you BASTARD." I was now looking for some aspirin to get over the pain. I so enjoyed watching Bob walk across the parking lot knowing that his lover was never going to show up. My pain gradually diminished, without any aspirin.

So, with the hysterics generally gone for the day, I was hoping to get back to my silence and solitude and get ready for the challenges yet to come. Being that Bob had never done a trip of this magnitude or experienced this level of isolation, I started to go over some of the details of what to expect during the trip. One of the biggest issues—no it's not the bears—it is your ability to mentally handle the fact that you have no immediate form of rescue, you have to rely upon yourself, your safety is strictly up to you, a mistake will cost you dearly if not kill you—you must understand that you have to be used to the fact that you will be uncomfortable most if not all of the time, and finally, you must fully be aware that everything is trying to kill you. This last fact alone brings pure honesty to every one of these trips as compared to what we all experience in the real world, which offers no truth. Don't forget that a bad or ill-prepared hiking partner is more deadly than any bear.

I truly tried to explain some of these important points to Bob, but it was apparent that his arrogance was not going to allow him to accept the truth without firsthand experience. So, I dropped the conversation and started to focus on some of the basics, such as gear, food, compasses, and clothing. Assuming that Bob was well covered, I forwent the gear check until we got into Port Alsworth. This proved to be a big mistake.

Later that day, we went shopping at the local Walmart. I was looking for light-weight foods in small packages to supplement what I'd brought from home. My goal was to keep my backpack below seventy pounds. Bob, on the other hand, was buying big, boxed items to take on the trip. Sure, it would be great to have a box of mac & cheese, canned soup, a box of cereal, and a two-pound bag of onions. Yes, fudging onions. The items that Bob was picking were as if he was going to an upstate New York campground for a weekend spree. NO! I told Bob this is not the way to pack for remote back country trips in Alaska. Did he listen? NOPE!!!

So, we got back to the hotel, and as we walked across the parking lot, Bob saw this girl and started talking to her. No, it wasn't the old lady. It appeared to be innocent, but my heart was in my throat, as I know the testosterone has not been released and that Bob is looking for something other than an innocent conversation. Sure enough, Bob got back to our hotel room about twenty minutes later and he was all excited saying, "This is the one, she likes me, I know it, and that she is staying on the second floor of this hotel." Bob opened the door of our hotel room with great vigor and said, "It's the third door on the right." I asked how he knew what door it was? He said he'd watched her go upstairs.

After about an hour of hanging out and getting stuff together for the trip, Bob stood up and said he was going up to her room. WHAT? WHY????? "Well, she does like me, you know." HOLY POOP!!! Here we go again!!!

Bob went up to her hotel door and started knocking. OH GOD HELP ME!!! After about ten minutes worth of knocking, there was no answer. About an hour later, we saw her in the lobby getting some snacks, and Bob approached her and started talking with her. I could see that she was getting nervous. I grabbed my snacks and went back to the room to watch some television. Bob returned about fifteen minutes later just aglow because of his new-found princess.

"So, what is her name?"

There was a pause, but no answer. He did not even know the name of his princess. I was truly getting concerned at this point, but I forced myself to refocus on the trip, my gear, and the adventures that were yet to come. As I was going through my food labels, I noticed that some ingredients included nut byproducts. Being that I am allergic to nuts, I got the packet of food and put it aside, offering it to Bob.

"So, what is wrong with this stuff?"

"Well, it has nuts, and I am allergic to nuts."

"Well how bad, you should eat nuts because they are good for you, and they contain protein."

"I know the benefits of nuts, but a reaction could be deadly."

"Well, let's see!" Bob grabbed some nuts and started rubbing them on my arm to see what would happen.

"What the FUDGE are you doing?!"

"Well, I want to see if you are allergic to nuts."

"I just told you I was."

I grabbed my allergy medication, took a swig, and hoped for the best. I did what I could not to beat the poop out of Bob.

In the meantime, Bob got up and said he was going back up to the girl's room.

"WHAT!? ARE YOU SERIOUS? YOU ARE GOING TO GET IN TROUBLE."

Despite my protestations, he went up and knocked on the door again with no answer. Bob came back to the room all dejected that he had not accomplished his quest.

"If you keep chasing her you are going to get us in trouble."

"NO. She likes me and wants to have a good time."

I was now counting the hours before we were to leave for Port Alsworth. Tiiiick toooock, tiiiiick tooooock, tiiiiiick toooooock. Time was moving way too slooooow!!

I told him to stop, but the following morning Bob saw her again and continued his inappropriate assertions. He went up to her room again!!! This was getting so out of hand, I was waiting to get arrested for these dumbass actions. Bob came back to the room in haste and said some guy answered the door and said that he was her boyfriend. The guy that answered the door was either her real boyfriend or her bodyguard. It was time to stop.

I was not having fun at this point at all; my silence and solitude were gone and my focus was now on not getting in trouble. Finally, the bush flight to Port Alsworth was getting near, so we had to concentrate on getting ready. It appeared the boyfriend had stopped Bob and the threat was over. Yeah right, but the question was could I get back into the mode of silence and solitude?

With about two hours left before our departure to Port Alsworth I saw Bob at the hotel computer, typing.

"What are you doing, writing your last will and testament before we leave?"

"No, I am writing a letter to the airlines that flew me up here."

"What the hell for?"

"Well, on the way up, I took my anxiety medication along with some alcohol while on the plane and I started acting a little strange."

"WHAT?!!!"

"So, when I landed after the first leg of my flight, they would not let me board my second flight."

"WHAT?!!!"

"They said I was acting strangely."

"WHAT!!!! So, this stewardess was an illusion?"

"No! She was real!"

"Are you sure?"

Survival on these types of trips requires self-reliance, self-respect, intelligence, a clear rational mind, and a sixth sense to stay out of trouble. Can a person with an overload of testosterone that is on anxiety medication and has a tendency to drink alcohol satisfy any of these requirements? What was going to happen when you added the elements of bears, freezing rivers, and complete isolation? I was scared to find out. What did the future have in store? How was Bob going to respond? Only time would tell, and I was truly concerned for our wellbeing.

I knew from past trips that the reality of the trip does not set in until you start taking those final steps of commitment. Loading your gear onto the float plane, flying over the vast emptiness of the Alaskan wilderness, seeing the foreboding valleys, mountains, large rivers, and finally standing on an unknown shore watching the last vestige of protection leaving as the float plane breaks its earthly bounds with the surface of the water, and gradually disappears in the mist of the sky. At this moment, you pause with great speculation, without belief, then turn toward the mountain before you take that first step into the unknown, pause again to turn back around, look into the mist-filled sky looking for the float plane that just dropped you off. You see nothing, and then you are hit with the reality that silence and solitude are all around you, which for some is the essence and truth of life, and for others is a living hell. A hell that is surrounded by truths that you wish to ignore in order to live a normal life.

So, what would happen when Bob got to this point in the trip? Would he relish the silence and solitude or be scared to face that he lives a normal life that cannot stand the truth that has always been before him…himself. At this point, he thought that he was greater than Mother Nature herself, that he could handle the great Alaskan outback like a walk in the Adirondack Park. I was truly concerned about his reaction and wellbeing at this point. I feared not the bears and weather yet to come, but I did fear the unknown when it came to dealing with Bob. Time would allay my fears or take me to the dark abyss of survival.

So, while I was reviewing Bob's dissertation, I looked up to gather my thoughts and, sure enough, I saw the "knock knock girl," the one who never answered her hotel door after Bob's knocks. She dropped her head immediately and left the lobby. I felt horrible for her— and embarrassed. I finished my review of Bob's dissertation, gathered my things, and waited outside for the taxi to the airport to catch the small plane to Port Alsworth. I was glad to be out of the hotel and was hoping that things would get back to thoughts of silence and solitude. To have expectations is always a bad thing that leads to broken hearts and dashed dreams. I made the mistake of having expectations that things would get better. I was absolutely wrong.

Port Alsworth is a beautiful town that is located in southwest Alaska. The only way to get to Port Alsworth is by taking an hour-and-a-half flight out of Merrill Field Airport. This is one of the most spectacular trips that you can ever take. The flight takes you through the Lake Clark Pass and you can see majestic mountains just off the tip of your wings, amazing valleys, glaciers spilling out of giant mountain valleys touching the rivers below, and wildlife such as bears, moose, and mountain goats. This flight alone really opens up your spirit by letting you feel the spectacular truth of Mother Nature.

What is even more impressive than the flights are the less than one hundred people that make Port Alsworth the town that it is today. This town was founded by the Alsworth family back in the late 1800s, and to this day, they have made it a place that embraces its small number of guests as if they are family. I had been to Port Alsworth several times before this particular trip and had garnered a bit of a reputation and respect from Glen Alsworth, his family, and the locals.

Based upon this reputation and past trips to Port Alsworth, I wanted to ensure that Bob was aware and that he would not under any circumstances try to hit on any girls and direct him to enjoy the beauty that is offered…and to simply look forward to the trip. While a little offended by my comments of caution, I had truly hoped that he would behave himself. With expectations—and you know how I feel about expectations—I settled back in my plane seat and closed my eyes, searching for silence and solitude. The silence and solitude of the flight were perfect as I enjoyed the thoughts of the trip to come and played over and over again some of the potential scenarios that could confront us. Some of the scenarios included an encounter with bears, bad weather, hypothermia, snow, rain, river crossings, and injuries, just to name few. I had bear spray, which is an aerosol containing chemicals that irritate your eyes, skin, and throat, so I had a false sense of security. I had a raincoat, but in Alaska it rains from the inside and outside, so you are always wet. Hypothermia was covered with my thirty-degree sleeping bag. River crossings would be easy if you followed the basic rule of facing the oncoming water when you cross, and by crossing at the widest place in the river. Everything else to be concerned about was a matter of luck, good decisions, and a whole lot of prayers.

I was jolted to full consciousness when the landing gear of the plane hit the dirt runway in Port Alsworth. I looked out the window and it felt good to be close to home again, a place where purity of the soul could be released without the destructive comments and expectations of others. I took my time getting off the small plane, and once I got to the cabin door, I stood up straight—something you cannot do in a small plane—took a deep breath, and felt at peace. I could not wait for the final flight into the wilderness, but that would have to wait until tomorrow afternoon.

Bob and I picked up our luggage off the dirt runway and started walking to our cabin on the shores of Lake Clark. During our walk over, I saw Glen Alsworth and some others that I knew in the distance and waved. Bob, on the other hand, saw a girl and her father walking along the runway headed toward Samaritan's Purse, which is an organization that takes care of American soldiers who have given their best to our country and gives the soldiers an opportunity to feel like they once felt before their lives changed forever.

"Pat, Pat, Pat...are you paying attention? Look! Over there."

"What are you talking about?!"

"See that girl? She is real pretty. I want to go talk with her."

"Hell, no. Leave her alone and keep it in your pants for a change."

Bob ignored me and waited for an opportunity, and before you knew it, he'd found a new target.

"Let's go check out our cabins and grab some lunch."

Bob actually followed! So, we got to the cabin, unpacked all of our gear to start the gear check, and then instead decided to take a five-mile hike up to Tanalian Falls to explore the area and some of the beauty that was soon to come. We took off on the hike, and every few minutes I would hear "Man, that is beautiful! Wow, look at this! Did you see that?" and "This place is amazing!" I thought Bob finally was getting into the spirit of the trip and that all of his ooooohhhhhs and aaaaaaaaaaahhs might be releasing some of his testosterone driven desires. A little expectation here!!! You know what I say about expectations!!!

As our hike continued, we finally broke into an open area that was being blessed by the rays of the sun, surrounded by pine trees, white mountain tops, giant boulders, and the constant glitter of water. The glittering of the water hits your eyes in a rhythmic manner, putting you into an instant trance that allows you to feel the spirit of what surrounds you and the progression of life as the it plummets over the falls and continues to move on to nourish. And for others, they simply cherish the view. This was a truly amazing place.

The reflection of the glittering water in my eyes was temporarily interrupted by a pair of boots jumping off the rocks into the water. I asked, and Bob said, "Look! it's that girl coming up the trail that I saw earlier. I am going to speak with her."

Well, I guess the ooooooohs and aaaaaaaahhs from earlier in the day did not take care of the problem after all. With a lurch, jump, and a bit of a sprint, Bob was on the girl within seconds. This situation was different because this girl was here with the father and was not interested at all.

Bob pursued and said, "Can I walk you to the edge of the waterfalls?"

The girl said, "I don't need any help."

I was cheering for the girl to swat the meandering mosquito (Bob) and tell him to get away. It came close, but she never told him to get away directly. From my point of view, this girl was looking for her own silence and solitude. I didn't see her mother, so maybe her mother had recently passed on, there was a divorce, or who knows what, but she wanted to be alone with her father. This attack ended fairly quickly, and I was happy to see that. Alaska for some is a getaway; for others it is a place to regain your soul and make peace with all that frustrates you.

So, with Bob once again rejected, we started our five-mile hike back to our cabin. This hike for the most part was fairly peaceful but for the fact that Bob was now focusing on his recent ex-wife.

"So, Pat, why do you think my wife left me?"

REALLY?!!! I said to myself. Why the hell did I care?

My trips to Alaska are to forget about the real world and just enjoy what wilderness has to offer. Peace, solitude, self-reliance, and life-changing challenges. The outback of Alaska strips away all social conventions, superficial issues, and leaves you with yourself and our creator. I engaged Bob in a conversation about some of his perceptions as to why his wife left him. I get the typical answers of "I did my best, I provided food, a nice home, and loved her the best way I knew how. I just don't understand." So, after about an hour of hearing his sad assertions, I asked Bob one question.

"Did you ever cheat on your wife?"

Bob never answered the question and never spoke of his sorrows about his wife again.

We got back to the cabin and had a great dinner at Glen Alsworth's lodge; they cook amazing dinners for their guests. We started to get serious about getting our gear together and arranging our backpacks. I organized things based upon need during the course of the day and packed non-essential stuff at the bottom of my backpack. Bob, on the other hand, was pulling out the food that he bought at Walmart: boxes, cans, long pepperoni logs, bags of potato chips, and other big stuff. He was throwing stuff at me saying, "Here, put this in your backpack." I looked at what was a box of mac & cheese.

I said, "This won't fit."

"Here, just do this." Bob crushed the box under his feet and said that now it would fit. He does this with about five or six boxes of stuff. This guy is crazy. This is not the way to pack for a trip in Alaska.

I shifted my focus to standard survival gear, like a small knife, spork, bowl, water bottle, raincoat, and trekking poles. I had all this organized so it all fit together in a manageable area within my backpack. Being that you always have to work as a team and not duplicate dual use items, I asked Bob what he had for gear. He pulled out a huge kitchen knife, full-sized spoons, and a large frying pan. WHAT THE HELL IS GOING ON? NO EXPERIENCE HERE!!! I was now looking for the kitchen sink along with the faucet. So, all of the big box stuff Bob flung at me, I put in the corner.

Bob said, "You are not listening to me. Take that stuff."

"Hell no! That stuff is too big and not meant for lightweight backpacking trips."

There were about twenty pounds of large items that I was not going to add to my pack. He also wanted me to carry his two pounds of fudging onions. Bears just love to have a little human meat along with some fine smelling onions on their human shish kabobs. Bob took his onions!!! Just in case you are not aware, one way to avoid contact with a bear, or to avoid bringing a bear into camp, is to suppress any unnecessary smells. This did not happen during our trip.

So, I finished packing my backpack, stood it up on the floor, stepped back, and admired its perfect form. I picked it up and the weight felt very reasonable. This is typically the case, but everything changes when you add your final supplies. Everything changes again when you are dropped off in the outback and fill your water bottles. This is the time to assess the weight and comfort of your backpack. Sure enough, I was close to seventy pounds. I sat next to my backpack watching Bob gathering his things and stuffing them into his backpack, which was barely suitable for this trip.

"How do you plan on fitting the pepperoni log into your backpack?"

Bob picked it up, held it in front of his crotch, and said, "This looks just like me."

Okay, so the stewardess, the knock knock girl, and the girl with her father all failed, so now he needed to compare himself to inanimate objects for satisfaction. I don't know, but if we saw a bear, Bob might be able to use his pepperoni stick to fend it off. Well, just maybe!!!

With the both of us packed, we took a look around the room to see what we might have forgotten. There was a stack of food and some other stuff, part of which Bob wanted me to take. With a little bit of distain, I heard, "Why aren't you taking that stuff?"

I quietly said to myself, *What? I am supposed to listen to an inexperienced hiker?* NOPE! The stuff was everything that Bob merely stepped on to make smaller. Like potato chips bags, which burst like a bomb all over the floor, mac & cheese, cereal boxes, and other stuff purchased at Walmart. On these types of trips, it is important to pack foods with high carbs, fats, and proteins, and to prepackage your daily snacks and dinners. I typically only eat one meal a day. This allows me to manage my pack weight that allows a reasonable amount of mobility in the event that I need to run. Yep, run!!! I never had to run away from anything. Thank God!!!

With the day getting late and dinner complete, we sat on the porch of the cabin talking about the trip, family, and other important things. The night before departure on these trips fills my mind with thoughts of what is truly meaningful in life. Some of my deepest acts of contemplation, especially on my solo adventures, end up not with what I could have done to improve and achieve my goals in life. Rather, my focus is on how many smiles I have left behind. I closed my eyes and thought of all the people that are smiling or have smiled because of me providing support, a little bit of love, bestowing confidence, or letting these people know they are important to themselves. I was once told by a great teacher in high school to look in the mirror every morning and say, "You are good, you are great, love yourself." I can envision this teacher saying that during class, and it has stuck with me ever since. I say those words every day. Every day that goes by, her words of encouragement evolve and grow as I meet other people. You see, I am who I am not because of myself but because of all those that I meet in life. Every person becomes a part of me. To love yourself is to infect others with love. My goal in life before I am recalled into the hands of God is to be a multi-billionaire. Not financially, but in the number of smiles others have experienced as the result of the love that I possess. My fear is not being able to pass on all that God has blessed me with. How many smiles have I left behind? My heart holds the truth, and God knows the number.

I opened my eyes, looked to the horizon, and saw the sun fading behind the mountains, casting the day's final hue of colorful light on the great pine trees, which were sparkling from the hue of light, the shimmering lake, and the faces of those that care enough to take a momentary pause to enjoy what is so simply made available to the world and our hearts.

"Patrick, do you know how long it has been since the last time I got laid?"

Well, I was really enjoying my thoughts, but in answering Bob's question, I said, "Do I really need to know?"

"Well, it has been longer than two weeks."

"Gee, that is a long time."

With so much going on in terms of Bob's antics and failed attempts, I was wondering if I was going to be safe during the course of the trip. More importantly, I asked myself the question of whether or not the wildlife was going to be safe. Was Bob going to fall in love with a bear or a moose? I could not wait to find out. Well, actually, I could! So, with the final vestige of light ebbing away in the sky I stood up, turned to the cabin, entered, took a look around, and with an ebb of confidence I thought *I am ready for what is yet to come.* I turned off the light and enjoyed the fleeting comfort of warmth. Tomorrow would come quietly and quickly but not soon enough.

I got up with the sun the following morning, and Bob and I went up to the lodge for breakfast. As per tradition, you always eat as much as is reasonably possible, for the food that is yet to come will be cold, lukewarm, and gag-worthy. There is something about these trips that really makes the gag reflex very shallow. Sometimes you insert the food, chew for a month of Sundays, then take a large gulp to get the food past the gag reflex. This is no easy task, but it is an essential one. I think that one of the problems is eating freeze-dried foods like eggs (GAG), or beef stroganoff (GAG). Okay! No more details here. I am really getting sick!!! OH, one more thought. I hate beans and anything with beans. A lot of the food on these trips contains beans, which is always an instant GAG with a lot of regurgitation. DONE!!!

Getting back on point, after a fine breakfast, ooooooh here comes a GAG. Well maybe I am not done yet, focus, focus, focus…Okay but anyway, we headed back to the cabin take our final controlled and manageable dumps and then just waited for Glen Alsworth to give us a signal when it was time to load the float plane and take off for Telaquana Lake. Typically, you have to wait for the morning fog to lift from both Port Alsworth and at Telaquana Lake. This is because most of the float planes, if not all, do not have radar-assisted flying. All the flying is done based upon visual sighting. The flight is about an hour and a half into the remote back country. The morning fog burned off and the sky initially turned blue. We were going to have a nice day. Glen then gave the nod. We grabbed our gear, loaded the plane, and with a rev of the engine we broke our earthly bonds and were headed into the unknown. Bob was really enjoying himself in the co-pilot seat, looking at all of the instruments and talking with our pilot, Glen. As we were flying out, I noticed the clouds to our north were getting dark. I looked to the south and also noticed what appeared to be a front moving in. The plane ride started to get a little rough. To determine the velocity of the wind, I looked toward the ground. As we passed over a lake, I noticed there were white caps. Those were big waves. So, we had weather coming in. We got to

Telaquana Lake and again I saw large white caps. I noticed Glen flying up and down the lake. He was looking for a good spot to land that had the least amount of wave activity. He spotted an alcove, throttled down, and started the descent. We skimmed the top of the water and initially it was smooth, but that was only because we had not made full contact with the water. Then bang, pop, bang, bang, bounce, shudder! Then we were bobbing up and down in the water. Glen's vast experience and knowledge as a pilot got us down safely. We grabbed the gear out of the plane and the storage compartments within the floats of the plane. We were now ready to start. As I repacked the bear spray, I noticed Glen calling me over.

"Patrick, we have an unprecedented storm coming into the area from the north and the south. This storm will produce strong winds in excess of sixty miles per hour, it will produce a lot of rain and in some spots, snow. I recommend that you guys spend some time getting up the mountain and find a low area to get away from the strong winds that should be here soon."

I knew something was up with the weather, but I did not realize the magnitude of what was yet to come. I thanked Glen and without delay he jumped in the float plane to get back to Port Alsworth before the storm got too bad.

I heard the engine of the plane and turned to watch

Glen take off as the mist generated from the prop of the plane hit me in the face. This is the point of transition when there is no going back. You are alone, and you drop from being the primary predator to becoming the hunted. This is a tough time for a lot of adventurers, especially new adventurers. How was Bob going to react? Well, it was time to find out. With Glen disappearing into the cloud-infested skies, we turned our attention to getting up the mountain to find a safe place to camp for the night. We grabbed our water bottles to fill them with water and added some purification tablets. The next spot to fill our water bottles was about a day and half away, so conservation of the water would be very important. This translates into our meals consisting of snacks and cold, dehydrated food. GAG! Hunger is not a problem once you get used to it. In reality, at least for me, you don't need half the food that you commonly eat when you are home, and when hiking I need even less than half. For some reason, my appetite disappears when I am on these adventures, and I only eat as required and when it is safe to do so.

With everything secure, I put on my raincoat, grabbed my pack, slung it onto my back, adjusted the shoulder straps, buckled the hip straps, and then tightened everything down nice and tight. It is important to minimize pack movement in order to reduce the effort it takes to move around, under, and over obstacles. My pack was heavy, but I knew it would be. I turned my attention to Bob and watched him gather some of his loose items and stuff them into his backpack, which was definitely stuffed full. He grabbed his pack, picked it up with a great deal of strain, threaded one arm though a shoulder strap and then another. He was already having a tough time. The right way to put on a pack is to grab it by both shoulder straps, pick it up, place the pack on your thigh, put one arm through a strap, get the pack to your shoulder and then feed your other arm through. This is the best way to handle a heavy pack. For Bob, this was something new, but he learned quickly as it was the easiest way to do things. With the both of us ready, we started our hike up the majestic mountain before us.

After about fifteen minutes, I turned to check on Bob to see how the pack was fitting and ensure that he was not lagging behind. I could see that he was having a hard time with the weight. We started off again and within a few minutes we just began to enter the alders. Alders, by the way, are shrub type plants that grow at the lower elevations in Alaska. They are very tall, thick, dense, and very, very hard to manage both physically and mentally. The best way to describe trekking through an alder field is to imagine doing thousands of push-ups, burpees, box jumps, high steps, get-ups, and resistance training all at once. It is very hard.

"Patrick, hold on for a minute."

"Bob, what is wrong?"

"Well, my pack is way too heavy, can you please take some of the weight?"

I knew this was coming at some point, but I did not think it would be this early. We were only twenty minutes into the trip.

"What do you need me to carry?"

"Well, can you please take my water bottles for now?"

Knowing what was yet to come, I agreed and took his water bottles. I knew more requests would be coming shortly.

As we entered the forest of alders, we were immediately tested by Mother Alaska. She assessed all who dared with an even hand, testing if they were strong enough to survive, or whether they would merely sit back in anguish and find reasons to give up and go home. A lot of adventurers use their families as an excuse for failure by saying, "I have failed them, they need me, I made a mistake being here." Pathetic! A true signal of failure is when you place demands on yourself that you must finish, "I have to do this," or, "I am a survivor and I am strong." These types of reactions indicate that your resolve as an adventurer is over and that you will take advantage of the next opportunity to go home. Bob had started down this path early.

After about thirty minutes of concentrated hiking, I

heard Bob.

"Patrick, can you slow down and wait for me! Please."

I did not realize that Bob was so far behind. I just kept my head down and tried to develop a rhythm of getting hit in the face by an alder branch, bend down, get on the stomach, crawl, jump up, pull branches out of the pack, and repeat. Bob was not yet in this rhythm and was expending a lot of energy fighting every branch. If you take your time and are willing to do the physical work, you can find a path of least resistance, but this takes good physical conditioning. To be in less-than-good shape will make you fight with the alders, which is sheer hell. After several hours of working hard and a couple of rest stops, we finally started to get above the tree line. At this point, we were walking on soft tundra and the brush was only as high as your knees. Easy walking is what I call it. This is one hell of a workout, but absolute fun. I could see that Bob was not enjoying the hell of the workout, but at least he was trying. His expectation was that he was going to be the king of the forest, king of the trip, and be a hero to all. Not so much, as he was now starting to realize a king has no throne in Alaska.

So, now above the tree line we now faced a new challenge. This challenge was that every step was like walking on a sponge, and it takes a great deal of energy to merely walk and that much more energy to walk uphill.

The best way to describe walking on tundra is walking in three feet of snow. Every step must be deliberate, high, and strategically placed. Not an easy task at all, but it is fun. After about four hours of hiking, we finally got to a point where the weather was getting worse and we needed to take shelter, as Glen Alsworth recommended. With only half the mountain conquered, I found a low spot, and we set up camp. The low spot would allow most of the strong winds to blow over us and hopefully keep the tent in one piece. It was too windy to cook any food, so we had snacks and a little bit of water. We still had another full day before we reached our creek-filled valley, so we had to be conservative with the water. With the sun just about gone over the horizon, I rolled out my sleeping bag, got in, and settled in for a good night's sleep. My only concerns were the weather and Bob. How was he going to do his first night in the wilds of Alaska? Well, a good night of sleep was not in the cards, as I stayed up most of the night tracking the weather, Bob, and listening for wildlife. The wind coming up the mountain was very intense, but we got lucky as the brunt of storm was not yet upon us. I was honestly hoping that it would miss us, but that would not be the case.

With a new dawn upon us, we grabbed some food, packed our gear, and set a path up the mountain. The best path was to head for the pass to the east. This would avoid the apex of the mountain and allow us to conserve some of our energy. It is very important on these back country trips to minimize the amount of energy needed to complete your day's task. In this case, the pass would be the best way to go.

It appeared from my standpoint that we could make the pass in about four to six hours, but in Alaska your expectations are never what they need to be. So, my realistic expectation was that we could reach the pass in about eight to ten hours, provided there were not too many false horizons. What is a false horizon, you ask? The best way to describe a false horizon is to compare it to an illusion. An illusion is something that you see, but is not real. Kind of like Bob, who is an illusion of a man…just kidding. Honestly, if you stand in front of a line of cars that are gridlocked on a highway, it appears the cars are all one solid line. If you started walking on top of the cars you would realize the line of cars are not connected and you would have to walk up and down each car. This is the way it is in Alaska. When you look up a mountain it appears to be a straight walk, but when you get up close you realize there are big valleys between your location and the top of the mountain. This makes it sheer hell, as you never know what to expect, but honestly this is part of the reason I like Alaska so much. Alaska teaches patience and respect, as we are not greater than the world we live in.

So, with the pass in view, we started hiking up the mountain at a reasonable pace and got a chance to enjoy some of the amazing scenery. At this point, you could see 360 degrees around you and well into the distance. In the distance, you saw beautiful mountains graced with white puffy clouds, and at times you saw the mountains blanketed in gold from the rays. At the base of the mountains there was a large lake, the lake that we landed on, which was a lot bigger than I imagined. It looked close from where I was standing, but it took about a day and a half to get to where my feet were currently planted.

After a few minutes of utter amazement, it was time to get moving. Time was precious when you had a lack of water and limited daylight. So, in about an hour or so we reached a plateau, which looked like a giant asteroid had hit and left a deep, bowl-shaped depression. After a brief assessment of the area, I decided to stay on the rim and walk along the outer edge. It was the long way around, but we were using less energy than walking down the crater and then back up the other side. Bob did not understand this and he headed down the crater. Energy is precious and should not be wasted.

Bob yelled and said, "What are you doing? Follow me."

I said, "Not a chance. The smart way to go is the easiest way to go." This is true in most cases.

Before Bob went too far, he realized the logic of what I was saying and hiked up to the rim and followed me to the other side. He was getting it!!! Well, maybe!!!

On the other side of the rim I saw a real nice surprise, a valley below with a river running through it. The river looked so small you could barely see the water. Translation! The river was still very far away, and there was a long way to go before we got water and camped for the night. Before we headed off the plateau, Bob and I decided to take a break and have a snack. During this time, I was doing an assessment of the area and noticed this plateau was surrounded by mountains and was the lowest point on the mountain range between the river and the lake behind us. I said to myself, *we have entered a pathway of least resistance,* which meant that this area was a wildlife highway. I got up, looked around and, sure enough, noticed bear scat. So, the bears that could not find food in the river would head over this plateau and to the lake to find salmon. Time to be careful and very alert. I checked my pistol, which was loaded, and made sure that I had easy access. To use a gun on a bear is usually a bad idea, because if you fail to hit and kill the bear with your first shot you stand a chance to get mauled and both you and the bear die in a big heap of mutilated flesh…and the other animals have a feast. Ouch, bad thought indeed. So, Bob was given a reasonable amount of warning to stay on the lookout for bears. I am not sure if he took me seriously, so I was doing double duty.

It takes a lot of energy to walk up hills with a backpack, but it takes almost the same amount of energy to walk down a hill. Why, you ask? Simple, because you have to control the weight on your back, which requires the use of a different set of muscles. The first thing to fatigue is your quads, your knees, your back, and then your feet, which take a ton of pounding. It was clear the day's hiking was catching up to us as our pace slowed going down into the valley. Once we hit the floor of the valley, we transitioned back into alders, but they were not as thick as those we'd experienced on the start of the trip. This was probably because the winter snowpack was deep, and temperatures were lower, all of which slow down the growth of vegetation. What is amazing is that a six-foot pine tree can be decades old. Things grow slowly in Alaska.

So, after finally getting to the river, I took a short pause and looked at what we'd traversed, and was amazed by the size of the valley and the massive mountains that surrounded us. It takes your breath away. With this moment taken in and committed to memory forever, it was time to get to the next challenge. Crossing the river. Why, you ask? To get to the other side of course. No chickens here!!! Ha ha!!!

As you know from my horrid experience near Turquoise Lake, crossing rivers in Alaska is a very dangerous task. If you fall in, you will learn that the chill of thirty-eight-degree water hurts like hell. The best way to describe it is like getting stuck with millions of needles all over your body at once. I mean, there is so much pain that your mind cannot process it, and you basically go numb immediately. I know how this feels because I made catastrophic mistakes in the past that resulted in serious injuries, some of which I still bear the scars of, both physically and mentally to this day.

So, to avoid the numbing situation of falling into the river, I looked over the area to find the widest place. The wider the river, the less likely the force of the water will knock you off your feet. After a bit of a debate with Bob, we finally selected a reasonable spot to cross. OH!!! There is more. When crossing, you must face the force of the water and look in the direction from where the river flows from. This gives you the best stability, provided you are not looking down at the flow of the water. If you do, you will become dizzy and lose your balance. So, heads up, and look up! Finally, if the current is bad enough, you will need to make a human chain with each person a little off center from the person in front of them. This way the person in front will breach the current as everyone else in the chain will hold the packs of the person in front of them and apply downward pressure to hold them in place. If the current is ever that strong, my recommendation is not to cross, just find a different route. To take your time in Alaska is to be smart, which equates to survival. Well, most of the time. After giving this detailed discussion to Bob, he merely blew it off and decided to do his own thing. Not smart, but he made it this time. The next time might be a different story.

With the tent set up and all our gear pulled out of our packs, we started a small fire and cooked some food. I am not sure what it is, but in Alaska after a hard day's work, it does not take much to satisfy one's appetite. The only thing I will not eat is beans. I really hate beans and anything that contains beans. I think I may have pre-gagged this earlier, but it never hurts to drive the point home once again. So, with the fire going it was nice to relax and enjoy the limited solitude of the surrounding mountains and think about those thoughts that only come once in a great while, and for some, once in a lifetime— if at all.

With the night slowly chasing out the remainder of the day's light, I noticed a change in the weather and wondered what surprises were coming the following day. Time will tell, so with a short prayer I got into the sleeping bag and gently closed my eyes, hoping to be graced with dreams that I had never experienced before. Then out of the blue, I heard the tent zipper, ruffling, and then I got a foot in the face as Bob got into his sleeping bag. Well, I did ask for an experience I'd never had before, and a foot in the face was it. Oh, the joy!

That night, as with every other night in the outback, I slept with one eye open. Besides paying attention to the wilderness and its majestic creatures, it was a fairly good night of rest. So, as I got up in the morning and as I was getting out of the tent, I mistakenly hit Bob in the head with my foot…NO! Just kidding, but the thought led to sounds of laughter echoing in the hills around me. With Bob getting up shortly thereafter, we prepared our unmemorable breakfast. Before sitting down for the food, I did my usual scan of the area, searching for wildlife. I looked to the east, where there was nothing but absolute beauty. I looked to the west and saw big mountains. I looked to the south and pondered what we would find, as that was the direction we were headed. I turned lazily to the north expecting the same results, but stopped. I looked once and then again. I saw movement. The movement of two little hairy fur balls that resembled tumble weeds, but tumble weeds do not exist in Alaska. For a few seconds, I was enjoying their playful movements. That ended very quickly when I saw the mother grizzly bear pop out of the brush. She looked at me, I looked at her, and quietly told Bob that it was time to go. Within a matter of minutes, we had the camp fully packed and we headed north. The grizzly was watching our every move, but she never saw us as a big threat being that she never postured herself in an attack position.

Remember what I said before about the mountain pass being a wildlife highway? Well, that was the direction she and her cubs were going. Up the pass and to the lake on the other side to catch some salmon. There was a good chance the grizzly and the two cubs passed through camp prior to me getting up. We got lucky, and I was happy about that.

As Bob and I continued our hike to the north, we must have turned and looked behind us a million times to ensure we were not being stalked in any manner. With the threat of the grizzly behind us, it was time to shift focus back to our trek. On that day, the plan was to hike down the valley and find a reasonable means of getting on top of the mountain to the west. This would prove to be a big challenge, as the mountains were very steep. To avoid some of these challenges, and to conserve energy, I decided we would walk down the valley for a couple of hours, as the farther down the valley we went the less foreboding the mountains seemed.

As the day continued, last night's concerns about the weather were coming true. I could see what appeared to be two weather fronts coming in from two different directions. This might have been one of the storms that Glen Alsworth had told us about, and it was.

The day progressed, the rains started, and the winds increased dramatically. The winds were so strong that the resistance generated from the wind made it hard to move forward. At one point, Bob and I were walking up a fairly large slope that was somewhat blocking the force of the wind. As soon as we got to the top of the slope, we were getting battered by the wind, and I mean battered. Kind of like a sky diver jumping out of a plane. Where there is an uphill there is usually a downhill, and we had a steep one to traverse.

Typically, when walking down a slope, you have to lean back to maintain your balance and control your backpack. On that day, this was not the case. When I started down the steep slope, and it was *steep,* I had to lean into the wind away from the slope. It was an amazing and very strange feeling. Several times as I was leaning forward, the wind gusts would subside and I would find myself falling, and then I would get caught by the wind again. This happened constantly for about an hour or so. It was actually fun for the most part and I looked forward to going through this again, but until that time we had some serious work to do as the weather was getting worse and the winds were getting stronger.

The constant rain and wind were relentless, and despite the intense amount of work that we were putting in to get to our destination, it was hard to maintain any real core heat within our jackets and rain gear. We were basically walking our way into hypothermia, which is a real killer while trying to reach our destination. With both Bob and myself suffering from chills, it was decided that we would set up camp on the side of a hill next to a small creek. A creek turning into a river. It was not a wade-the-water crossing, it was more of a balancing act, bouncing from stone to stone. Before we started to cross this creek, I heard, "Bob is hungry, Bob wants food." I just about pissed my pants over the fact that Bob wanted to stop and have something to eat. Here we were during a storm and immersed in alders, and Bob wanted food. It is extremely dangerous to be in a stand of alders, not being able to see what is around you or coming at you. With Bob feeding himself, I was very alert and listening to every sound. Up the creek, I heard a snapping branch not once but a couple times. I ran to my backpack, grabbed my Smith & Wesson 50 caliber pistol, got in position and pointed the gun in the direction of the sounds. Bob heard and saw all of my activity, dropped his food, and ran up to me saying, "Protect me, protect me!"

"Well, get the hell out of my way!"

Bob's fear consumed him. I said to get prepared to put on your backpack and let's start moving again. Within minutes, both packs were on. I saw nothing coming our way, so whatever had made the noise was probably scared by all of our commotion. A second close call.

With the threat of hypothermia upon us, we decided to make camp about an hour away from the creek. This proved to be a good idea, as the weather continued to get a lot worse. We set up the tent on the side of a hill between two large rocks to provide some additional shelter. With the weather so bad, there was no way to light a fire or even use our camp stoves. So, we had a great cold dinner of pepperoni and other random snacks. Once we stuffed our stomachs, it was time to wait for the storm to blow ever.

With the wind and rain pounding our now-leaking

tent, I decided to get my belt buckle and wrap it around the tent poles that crossed at the top to stop the tent from being torn apart. To hold onto this strap was a challenge, but if the tent ripped or were destroyed, we would be in serious trouble, as rescue is never immediate in bad weather despite the fact that we had the Garmin. My true concern was keeping our sleeping bags dry. If they get wet, you have no place to go to get warm. So, with the storming ripping, I got into my sleeping bag and got ready for a long stay. When you get into situations like this, you have to be at peace with yourself in order to enjoy the solitude of the mind and the music of the wind. Those that are not settled within themselves typically cannot handle isolation, the rhythm of the wind, and their thoughts of potential disaster. To settle the mind is a true accomplishment, as it brings peace to one's life. The wind and rain were playing a beautiful melody that made my heart dance. I was having a good time.

A couple of hours in to the solitude, I could see that Bob was getting restless and fidgety. He was playing with the zipper on his sleeping bag. Pulling it up and down, up and down. A couple hours later I heard the famous words, "Bob is hungry, Bob wants food." He grabbed an onion and started eating it like an apple, bite after bite.

I said, "What in the hell are you doing?"

"I am hungry!!!"

The deal in bear country is not to get killed by a bear and to decrease the chance of drawing a bear into camp. You never eat where you are going to sleep and you minimize the odors as much as possible.

"Don't you understand?!!!"

"Well, it's only an onion. And I love onions."

"OH MY GOSH!!!! You are going to get us killed. Put that onion away and back into a sealed bag. Stupid is as stupid does."

There was no common sense here at all! Oh, what have I done! Hours later, Bob said that he wanted to send a message to his family. "Can I use your GPS unit?"

I said, "Sure, but don't forget that is our only source of connection with the real world and rescue, if needed. So, keep it short and don't burn out the batteries."

Well, after about an hour of tinkering with a text message, Bob said, "Should I use the word 'adventure' or 'journey,' which one sounds more poetic?"

"WHAT! I SAID KEEP IT SHORT."

Half of the battery's life was gone. Ignorance is truly bliss. I told Bob to send his message and shut the GPS off. He rebuked, but I insisted, as we were only on the second day of our trip and we had a long way to go.

More time went by and we were still holed up in our tent and my good buddy said he had to take a pee, but it was still raining outside. I told him to put on his rain coat and get it done. Bob got on his knees, unzipped the tent, and took a piss right in the area that we crawl to get out of the tent.

"What in the hell are you doing? Take the walk and get away from the tent!"

"Oops, I am already done."

Only a fool is willing to crawl through their excretions to get into and out of a small tent. What was going to happen when he had to take dump? Would he shit in his sleeping bag or in the tent? I was truly concerned. It is very important when doing outback adventures that you maintain your health and wellbeing.

So, when it comes to hygiene, you must always keep your hands clean, eating equipment clean, and make sure that you do not share food, as you might have contaminated hands. To make a mistake in the outback will result in experiencing the wrath of Mother Nature. Not good! Bob was oblivious to these key points.

After a few more hours went by, the night gripped our surroundings as the wind and rain continued to batter the tent. The strength of the wind was gauged by my belt that was tied around my hand and the top of the tent. The harder the wind blew, the higher my hand bounced. If my hand was swinging back and forth it meant the wind was blowing up the valley, which was very bad. If my hand was bouncing and swinging at the same time, it meant the tent was on the verge of being torn apart. All this made it virtually impossible to sleep, as every time I closed my eyes I was fiercely interrupted by violent gyrations of my hand and sounds of wind that emulated that of a train going through your living room. It was intense. I made a final attempt at some sleep, but then a gyration of my hand was accompanied by a spray of water. Holy poop, the tent was now starting to leak and our gear was starting to get wet. I found the rip in the tent and tried to make some adjustments, but the rain continued to find its way into the tent. So, we moved our gear and kept as much of our stuff as dry as possible.

We were now approaching eighteen hours of being inside our tent, weathering this storm. All seemed to be fairly quiet. Then, like an atom bomb going, off Bob sprang up, stuck his head out of the top of the tent and said, "WEEEEEEEE LOOK OUTSIDE!" This scared the hell out of me. I panicked and asked myself, *did Bob lose it?* I looked outside myself, and the weather was still fairly bad. A couple hours later, the wind died down and we were finally able to go outside, eat some food, and pack up our wet gear. What really concerned me was that later in the day I asked Bob about his "WEEEEEEEE" moment and he did not remember sticking his head through the tent.

Our goal was to hike up to the plateau that heads

toward Turquoise Lake. Once we reached the plateau after a couple hours of steep hiking, the sight was amazing, as all of the mountains around us had gone from a wet-looking grey to brilliant white. The storm that we just experienced turned out to be an August snowstorm in the upper elevations. After a breath break before entering the plateau, I signaled to Bob that we would be proceeding east. The route looked fairly easy, but my experience told me otherwise. I anticipated that it would take us about eight hours to get to the point where we could see Turquoise Lake.

As we proceeded with our day's adventure, the skies were still overcast and there was a light rain, which was enjoyable compared to what we'd just experienced. What made this hiking more difficult than hiking up to the plateau was all of the tussocks. What is a tussock, you ask? Well, tussocks are vegetation that grow in tall clumps ranging from a couple inches to a couple of feet tall. What makes tussocks challenging is the fact they grow in close proximity, making it nearly impossible to walk around them or on top. You typically have to step up and down, up and down. Doing this for hours is tough work. What made this even more fun was the fact that there was water between most of the tussocks. The challenges never stop, but that is what makes Alaska fun.

As we were hiking along, I detected that Bob was getting a little frustrated and tired from all the work. I asked, "What's up?"

He said in a high pitched voice: "MY FEET ARE WET, I DON'T LIKE WET FEET."

In retort, I said, "Well, you are in the back country of Alaska. Did you expect to have dry feet?"

Bob whined like a little kid and we continued. A few minutes later, Bob said, "No, you are going the wrong way. If we go north toward the mountains, it will dry my feet and make for better hiking."

I said, "Not a good idea, as the walking does not get easier, nor dryer, plus you are walking into the snow and colder temperatures."

During this discussion, Bob kneeled on the ground, put his hands in a small, stagnant pool of water, and started drinking.

"Stop, you fool! That is stagnant water. You never drink stagnant water, only moving water."

He did not understand the threat of Giardia and the fact it could kill you if contracted in the remote wilderness. Another potentially costly mistake. With Bob's frustration still growing, he wanted to go north toward the mountains, despite the fact it was in the wrong direction. I told him no and continued on my designated path toward Turquoise Lake. I noticed after a few minutes that Bob had decided to head north on his own. I knew it was a mistake, but I decided to let him learn on his own. After about an hour or so and with Bob almost vanishing into the mist, I noticed that he'd changed course and started heading back in my direction. Once he was back in earshot, I said, "What have you just learned?"

"Well, I know that it is not easier walking and my feet are not dry."

I was hoping that he was humbled by his mistake, but to no avail. Alaska is not kind to those who think they are greater than its grandeur. So far, so lucky.

With Bob back in line for the moment, we continued to head toward Turquoise Lake, sometimes stepping on top of tussocks, other times between, and other times up and down, up and down. I made up a game for myself to see how many tussocks I could walk on top of until I had to step down. What made this game a lot of fun was that every tussock was a different size and sometimes my foot would fit on top and other times there was barely enough room for one of my feet. So, with one foot in the air, trying to balance long enough to find your next tussock step was a rip. It was like walking on a wiggly tight rope. I would recommend this game to anyone that goes to the Alaskan back country.

After a good couple of hours of hard tussock work, I noticed the plateau was starting to slope down, meaning that we were getting close to the river basin and Turquoise Lake. I looked up, focused on the horizon, and saw black spots that I used as my navigation points. I took another moment and gazed at all that was around me, hoping to see Caribou, bears, or some other form of life. All that I saw was a flicker of a Caribou running through the mist, but I never saw the entire herd. It was very mystic and cool to see that one Caribou.

As time went by, my navigation points kept on changing in shape as they got bigger and bigger, and a lot more appeared. I was deeply curious and could not wait to explore these unknown shapes. As we got closer, these black spots became very impressive as they were very tall, thin rocks that were sticking straight out of the ground. It almost appeared as if someone placed them there purposely. The best way to describe what I was seeing was like seeing Stonehenge. There appeared to be logic as to their placement, as there were no other formations like this on the plateau. Okay, maybe, just maybe, these formations were placed by aliens a long time ago to attract other aliens. I know stupid is as stupid says. Well, maybe not, as an asteroid in the 1940s hit this area and left a crater. I asked the locals in Port Alsworth and the National Park Service personnel to show me the location on a map, but they all refused. I even did some research before leaving on this trip to find the location and could not do so. Alien…wait, I see one…OH! It's Bob. Just kidding!

As we were walking through the Alaskan

Stonehenge, some of the rocks and the way they were lying made perfect caves. You could see the backs of some, and others were deep enough that you could not see the end. There was a great passion to explore all of these caves, but my instinct told me there was a good possibility of finding bears or wolves in the caves. So, with great caution, we walked through the rock field and continued our trek down into the valley. At one point, we found a big, round bolder and decided to use it as wind break during lunch, as the wind that had been moderate all day long was starting to pick up again. Our lunch break was short, as the wind cooled us down rapidly and we both started to get cold. So, we hoisted the packs and continued into the valley below.

After a long day of a fun and exciting hiking, at least for me, we decided to make camp in a pretty random spot. Random meaning there was not a real close water source, but the lake was in view. All we had was what was in our bottles. Not only did the wind pick up, but the rain went from a drizzle, like it had been all day, to a heavy rain. During one of the wind gusts, I faced the wind, stretched out my arms, and enjoyed the breeze and rain hitting my face. When I did this, Bob thought I was crazy, but the freedom of spirit that you experience when the winds of Mother Nature flow through your arms, legs, and around your head, it lifts you and creates the ability to soar to places far beyond. Even to this day when the wind is blowing hard outside at my Upstate New York home, my spirit is immediately lifted and I am on my way.

After we got our tent set up and our gear laid out, it was obvious that Bob was less than comfortable. So, to get warm, Bob attempted to start a fire by gathering some brush, as there were no trees available. He piled it up and tried several times, using a lighter to start the fire. The wood was too wet, the wind too strong, and the rain was falling too hard. So, after several attempts, I gave Bob my small spray container of hand sanitizer and told him to spray the wood. Every time, the wet twigs would erupt into flames and go out immediately. A fire was not going to happen on this day. So, we got into our sleeping bags and finally got warm. During our conversation, Bob kept saying, "Why are we in Alaska? The Adirondacks in New York are the same. Why am I here?" Bob said this about twenty times that night. This was a clue that his resolve to challenge himself and Alaska's great outback was waning. This had me concerned, as there was really no easy way out if the weather did not change.

Early the next morning, Bob once again sat up rapidly, squealing in a high-pitched voice, "Get me out of here, I want to go home. Now! Get me out of here. Give me your satellite phone." Bob had finally lost it completely. Alaska was not the place for Bob. So, out of fear for Bob, and with a great deal of hesitation, I called Glen Alsworth and asked if he could pick us up on Turquoise Lake. Glen Alsworth is a true hero to a lot of hikers as he has saved many over the years. After I called Glen, I called Joanne to let her know what was going on and that Bob wanted to go home.

Bob said, "Why did you tell Joanne I wanted to go home?"

I said, "It's my wife, and I don't lie to my wife."

So, with Glen coming in the late afternoon, we had to get moving in order to meet him on the opposite shores of Turquoise Lake. This would take some time. The part that I was most worried about was crossing the drainage basin with Bob. We finally got to the drainage area, and the river was fairly wide with fast-moving water. We walked along the river for a while and finally found the best spot, which was better than some of the other areas, but still not ideal. I gave Bob another tutorial about how to cross and be safe. I don't think that he listened at all. We made our first attempt, but the river was too swift and deep, so I moved us farther down the drainage. This second spot was wider but still very dangerous. I decided to go back toward the lake and try a new spot that looked promising. I took off my boots and put on river shoes, unbuckled my waist and chest strap, and start moving into the river. The first half was fairly simple and went without a problem. The second part of the crossing was the dangerous part. As we moved across the river, we made a couple of tries, retreated, and tried another spot. Bob lost his cool once again and this time said, "I just want to go across now and I am going." I tried to stop him, but not a chance. Bob hit a deep spot in the river, one I tried to avoid, and sure enough the current was too strong. He got pulled under and flailed in the cold water trying to regain his feet. If Bob had followed me another fifteen feet up the river he could have made it without a problem. I rushed across the river with only wet knees, got to the bank across from Bob and assisted him in getting out of the river. Bob, freezing his ass off, stripped as instructed and put on dry clothes. Bob was lucky that his impatience did not create a more dangerous situation. After he was situated, I gave him a hug and we continued along the banks of the Turquois Lake and finally got to Glen's pickup point.

With time on our hands, we set up the tent, pulled out some gear, got comfortable, and made some food. After about an hour or so, the sun came out and highlighted the mountain before us and set sparkles across the lake. It is quite amazing when these moments arrive, but usually they are short lived, as the weather in Alaska changes every five minutes.

With the sun ablaze, Bob said, "I want to go climb that mountain. Pat, call Glen and cancel our pickup. I want to stay longer."

"WAIT!!! A couple of hours ago in the tent you FREAKED and wanted to go home."

I knew that Bob's aspiration of climbing the

mountain was unreasonable and the adversity of doing so would result in Bob having additional relapses. We had been lucky up to this point and based upon what I had seen and experienced, the smart play was to take Bob back to civilization and have him go home. I was not going to take another chance.

We heard an engine, looked in the sky, and saw a blue and white Cessna float plane. We quickly packed up our gear, helped Glen gently bring the plane to shore, loaded our gear, and headed back to Port Alsworth. The sequence of packing our gear, putting the gear into the plane, hearing the engine come to a roar, the floats skipping along the surface of the lake, then hurtling through the skies and watching the mountains, rivers, and valleys pass under me, was spiritual. The truth and honesty of Mother Nature was being left behind, once again, with every passing moment. I tried to hold on to the honesty, but as soon as we touched down on Lake Clark, I knew the fantasies of honesty and truth would not be experienced anew until I was once again in the outback of Alaska.

We got off the plane, walked to our cabin, and relaxed for a few, then got back into the social flow of the world. We had a night at Port Alsworth and then the following day Bob made arrangements to fly back to Anchorage and home to Philadelphia. I was not interested in going back so soon, so I stayed in Port

Alsworth for a few more days to get over the stress of the trip and taking care of Bob. After this trip ended, Bob, who thought of himself as the savior and king of Alaska, was humbled and embarrassed, as he thought Alaska would be like the Adirondacks. Bob and I never talked much about the trip after it ended, but I can understand that he did not want his family and friends in Philadelphia to know how bad it was and the fact that his fear of the unknown and being alone was hard to handle.

Story 5

The Adventurer's Nightmare

During every trip, there are moments that lead you into a different Realm, change your life forever, and leave you in a state of undefined expectations. These moments can come at any time and are sometimes sparked by the environment around you. Most of us know of this Realm but have chosen to ignore and simply forget that it even exists. It takes a brave and self-trusting person to place themselves in a situation that brings the slightest chance of slipping into this Realm of life that can bring happiness, sadness, or nothing but sheer hell.

What in the hell am I talking about? Well, I will try to explain through a series of those moments that I've had over the years. Some are pretty easy to talk about, but others are extremely deep, confusing, and unexplained.

On my very first trip into the back country of Alaska, I was dropped off by a float plane in the middle of nowhere, and I was not to be picked up for a couple of weeks. My pick-up point was a lake about 120 miles away. I remember the excitement of planning this trip;

buying the gear, stepping onto the plane in my hometown, and stepping off the plane in Anchorage. All these initial steps, without my knowledge, were pushing me toward The Realm of which I knew but did not understand. This was a very strange feeling, but I continued without abatement. When it was time for me to board the plane from Anchorage to a small bush town of only a few residents, things began to get more interesting, as I was about to take the leap into a new world. When I got on the float plane to take me to the remote lake in the middle of nowhere, reality was no longer in the distance, but was enveloping me rapidly.

When I stepped off the plane at the remote lake and then watched the plane lift off and disappear into the distance, I knew I was facing The Realm of the unknown as the world of similarities was one hundred percent gone. The Realm was all around me and there was no easy way of going back physically or mentally. Nor did I want to go back, as I now knew that my heart would never return to what it once was before I entered this wilderness Realm.

I was hiking for days, sinking deeper and deeper into The Realm, enjoying the challenge, the mountains, streams, animals, everything. Then, on this one particular day, I was hiking up this large mountain, crested the peak, and on the other side there was a large patch of scree that felt like silk under my feet. I decided to sit down in this very spot. So, I took off my backpack, sat down, wiggled my butt into the scree, and buried my feet firmly. The view was amazing; I could see mountains, ranges, tundra, a river running out of the glacier filled valley above. I was overcome by everything. My mind was filling up with thoughts. Some sorrowful and others with questions about my sanity. Just kidding. Questions about how all natural things spur thoughts only found in The Realm. What came to me on this day was how I fit into The Realm. Am I a stranger in this place? Who else is in this Realm? I looked hard but did not see anyone else. I am not sure I wanted to see anyone. I was glad to be alone in the wilderness, and glad to be alone in this place I called The Realm. I guess the saying is true. That a strong heart thrives on loneliness and unresponsive echoes. I enjoy The Realm and hope to frequent this place more and more. It was so dang peaceful in this place that I did not want to move an inch. So, for just a little while longer, I laid back in the scree, stared at the sky, and listened to Mother Nature's songs being sung by the winds flowing through the pine trees, whistling through the mountains, and chasing the water running down the mountains. It was so cool, this place. I knew that I could not stay here forever, so as I stood up to continue, I took a couple of steps, stopped and turned to look at the butt and footprints that I'd left in the scree. I knew they would eventually fade into time, but I knew for sure that a piece of my heart would always live at this spot which took me fully into The Realm for the very first time. As I write this part of the book, I can feel my heart in this place, and it brings great joy and sadness because I am not there now. I hope that I will go back someday, but if not, I will continue to visit this place, like I have been, by closing my eyes, which allows me to travel back to the wilderness and the spots where I left a piece of my heart and enhanced my life. I personally call this "Traveling," as I can close my eyes and within seconds be at a place my heart desires. This is a beautiful, temporary thing, as it almost allows me to enter The Realm instantly and search for more meaningful things, but it is not enough to satisfy my adventurous soul. An adventurer needs full entry into The Realm to satisfy their passion. Without this full immersion, it is impossible to control the endless, constant draw of The Realm. It never goes away. It is for this reason that my heart is always compelled to meet its mistress, which is the mountains of my adventures past and the adventures yet to come. There must always be an adventure in the making, otherwise the world begins to fade.

Despite the fact that I had a spiritual intuition that The Realm existed, I now know it is as real as the wilderness is wild. My heart lives not in the world as we know it, but in The Realm. This makes it hard at times. Hard because I know there is a better place of which I cannot get to one hundred percent of the time. This is hard for sure. I never really knew being an adventurer would create such a worthy conflict.

Silence & Solitude

A lot of people, especially my family, really don't understand why I am so compelled to take solo trips in some of the most remote parts of Alaska, and they will probably never really know the full truth, as I don't know the full truth. That's okay, as an adventurer's true aspirations are spoken and never really understood. I have been asked on several occasions by friends, passengers, and short-term acquaintances why I take such crazy, dangerous trips. What is so compelling? I have given countless explanations, but none really seem to satisfy the inquisitor. They merely walk away, classify me at times as a fool, and in one case as a selfish son of a bitch. I generally don't respond to such comments, as those with such harsh words are themselves lost in regards to their journey and destination. I just let it go and pray they will one day find their path. If they don't, tough shit!

The one truth that most people might understand is the silence and solitude that comes with being totally alone in the wilderness. You see, silence and solitude bring with them great thoughts and a sense of what defines us as a person and brings to us those that we have lost over the years. It is also a place that provides a full release from all that binds us.

Whenever you walk out your front door, you are being judged, classified, and conditioned. Even within your own doors, judgment takes place and conditioning comes in the form of television and those things that surround us. What provides us entertainment is in reality a tool to reach socialized mediocrity. There are freedoms in this judgment, but a managed freedom that is comprised of well-constructed, orchestrated systems. Most of us have no problem with this, but more than most have no real understanding of what is happening. Most do not want to know.

Those that try to avoid the wilderness due to the lack of physical and mental comfort offered by Mother Nature are not equipped to reach into the realm of silence and solitude. For the wilderness is a conduit into The Realm. A place that has a means of reaching into your soul. A reach that comes from yourself without abatement. You are who you are, and no one else needs to know or understand. Remain true to yourself. So, I ask all that possess the strength, and the heart of God to live in this world with the comprehension of what is offered in The Realm. I know The Realm quite well, and I try with all of my heart to let others know the joys of The Realm and what it means. A great offering of The Realm is the fact that you are not only surrounded by the wilderness, but you are also surrounded by those that have loved you in the past and have gone on to better places. Just think for a moment about all of the people you have met during your life. Think about what they have done as your friend or foe. You will find you have taken pieces of these people, which have assisted in making you what you are today. Some of the many parts that made me who I am today come from my family and friends. So, I walk, talk, and live life, not based upon myself, but on all those that have surrounded me and touched me over the years. The sum of my greatness is everyone else but myself. The Realm is a place of true love and shows you the sum meaning of life. So, love thyself so you can love others and therefore yourself.

So find your silence and solitude and cherish what it means to you and the feelings that surround you. Don't get lost in self-doubt, otherwise you will forever be a lost soul.

This story has come to an end for now. God bless and love to all!

www.ingramcontent.com/pod-product-compliance
Lightning Source LLC
Chambersburg PA
CBHW021622120626
46545CB00001B/348